Monetary Equilibrium and Nominal Income Targeting

T0331479

This book examines the case of nominal income targeting as a monetary policy rule. In recent years the most well-known nominal income targeting rule has been NGDP (level) Targeting, associated with a group of economists referred to as market monetarists (Scott Sumner, David Beckworth, and Lars Christensen among others).

Nominal income targeting, though not new in monetary theory, was relegated in economic theory following the Keynesian revolution, up until the financial crisis of 2008, when it began to receive renewed attention. This book fills a gap in the literature available to researchers, academics, and policy makers on the benefits of nominal income targeting against alternative monetary rules.

It starts with the theoretical foundations of monetary equilibrium. With this foundation laid, it then deals with nominal income targeting as a monetary policy rule. What are the differences between NGDP Targeting and Hayek's rule? How do these rules stand up against other monetary rules like inflation targeting, the Taylor rule, or Friedman's k-percent?

Nominal income targeting is a rule which is better equipped to avoid monetary disequilibrium when there is no inflation. Therefore, a book that explores the theoretical foundation of nominal income targeting, comparing it with other monetary rules, using the 2008 crisis to assess it and laying out monetary policy reforms towards a nominal income targeting rule will be timely and of interest to both academics and policy makers.

Nicolás Cachanosky is Assistant Professor of Economics at Metropolitan State University of Denver, USA. His main research is on monetary policy and appears in the *Journal of Institutional Economics*, the *Quarterly Review of Economics and Finance*, and in the *Review of Financial Economics* among others.

Routledge International Studies in Money and Banking

For more information about this series, please visit www.routledge.com/series/SE0403

Monetary Equilibrium and Nominal Income Targeting

Nicolás Cachanosky

Routledge
Taylor & Francis Group

LONDON AND NEW YORK

First published 2019
by Routledge

2 Park Square, Milton Park, Abingdon, Oxfordshire OX14 4RN
52 Vanderbilt Avenue, New York, NY 10017

Routledge is an imprint of the Taylor & Francis Group, an informa business

First issued in paperback 2020

British Library Cataloguing-in-Publication Data
A catalogue record for this book is available from the British Library

Library of Congress Cataloging-in-Publication Data
Names: Cachanosky, Nicolás, 1981- author.
Title: Monetary equilibrium and nominal income targeting / Nicolás Cachanosky.
Description: 1 Edition. | New York : Routledge, 2018.
Identifiers: LCCN 2018006651| ISBN 9781138215023 (hardback) | ISBN 9781315444604 (eBook)
Subjects: LCSH: Monetary policy. | Banks and banking. | Income--Econometric models.
Classification: LCC HG230.3 .C33 2018 | DDC 339.5/3--dc23
LC record available at https://lccn.loc.gov/2018006651

ISBN: 978-1-138-21502-3 (hbk)
ISBN: 978-0-367-58944-8 (pbk)

Typeset in Times New Roman
by Sunrise Setting Ltd, Brixham, UK

To the memory of Juan Carlos Cachanosky

Contents

Illustrations

Figures

Table

Acknowledgements

I am grateful to a number of colleagues who, through a number of years, have contributed to shape the ideas presented in this book. Colleagues who I think have been more influential are Larry H. White, George A. Selgin, William Luther, Thomas L. Hogan, and Alexander W. Salter. Without continuous interaction with them the idea and structure of this book would have never taken place. Two names deserve a special mention: Adrian O. Ravier, who tirelessly incentivizes me to put into words our lengthy discussions; and Andrew T. Young, who in the Spring of 2015 held a workshop on the topic of "Should Central Banks Target NGDP?" at West Virginia University (United States). The paper presented at that workshop became the germ idea of this project.

Routledge also deserves a grateful recognition for not only providing support in the production of this text, but also for their encouragement and trust in inquiring if I would be interested in writing on this topic. Thanks to their support, what initially was a draft of a paper presented at a workshop is now a book on the topic.

Introduction

Just as it seemed to be the case that central banks learned how to execute a monetary policy that would yield low output volatility and low inflation, a financial crisis of historic proportion shattered the economic quietness of the Great Moderation. Until it was too late, such a financial crisis was unforeseen by major central banks around the world. And as the crisis unfolded, central banks seemed to be more running behind the events than advancing future problems. In addition, during the crisis, central banks were seen moving away from *conventional* monetary policy and entering the realm of new and unexplored *unconventional* policy making.

The misdiagnosis of the economic imbalances that were being built in addition to the exploration of a new and an *unconventional* way of doing monetary policy invited a revision, among other questions, of what a central bank should do to guarantee economic stability. It should be patent now that price level stability is not a synonym of monetary stability. Among these revisions the proposal of central banks targeting nominal gross domestic product (NGDP) gained momentum. While admittedly the topic of targeting nominal income is not *new*, and goes back at least to the early twentieth century, the economics profession has started to pay more attention to this old and forgotten proposal since 2008. This book deals with this specific issue, and how monetary equilibrium is the guiding principle behind nominal income targeting. This book does not question the presence of central banks, it rather takes them as given and studies why these institutions should move their focus away from price level stability toward nominal income. Whether or not central banks are as needed as it is usually assumed is an interesting area of research that is not part of this manuscript. Still, some institutional reforms of different degrees are presented in the last chapter.

A question like the one presented in this book requires, first, consideration of what should be used by central banks as a benchmark of monetary policy. This is the topic of the first chapter. This benchmark is: how does a free market of money and banking (free banking) work and what is the monetary outcome? This chapter presents the dynamics that take place under free banking that yield both monetary and financial equilibrium without particular need of a central bank to guarantee such equilibrium. Some of the most common objections to free banking are also contrasted in this chapter with the aid of a summary of events under two historical cases of this monetary regime. The market outcome of a free banking regime is a monetary equilibrium that can be interpreted as a stable nominal income or NGDP (per capita).

Chapter 2 moves from knowing how monetary equilibrium is achieved under free banking toward studying the distinctive characteristics of a stable nominal income. As is usually the case in this topic, this analysis is presented in terms of the equation of exchange. Of particular interest is the relation between nominal income and price level stability, and under which conditions these two objectives are equal to each other. That nominal income targeting does not focus on price level stability does not mean that inflation is of no concern. It means that nominal income targeting is able to distinguish between the effects on the price level of nominal shocks and real shocks. Nominal income targeting distinguishes between *good* (benign) and *bad* (malign) inflation and deflation. By definition, inflation targeting aims at stabilizing the price level, not nominal income. To the extent that a policy maker is trying to distinguish what type of inflation or deflation they are facing (a nominal shock or a real shock), they are in fact following a nominal income prescription. In this sense, nominal income targeting should not be a fringe idea to policy makers.

After discussing nominal income targeting in more detail, Chapter 3 moves to study the most familiar monetary rules, from Friedman's k-percent to Taylor's rule, including McCallum's feedback rule and the problem of discretion versus rules in monetary policy. With nominal income targeting as a benchmark, the focus of the chapter is how these monetary rules deviate, if they do, from targeting monetary equilibrium.

It is also possible that a central bank chooses the right tool but the wrong target. This is the topic of Chapter 4. In particular, what would the effects be should a central bank target a too high nominal income growth rate? In other words, what would a *too loose* monetary policy executed under nominal income targeting look like. A relevant case is when an expansionary monetary policy occurs with inflation absent, as arguably was the case in the years prior to the 2008 crisis. A few examples of why an excess of money supply may not result in higher price levels (at least soon enough) is also a discussion topic of this chapter.

However, the issue of choosing the right rule and the right target are not the only challenges faced by central banks. It is not the same to arrive at nominal income stability through monetary policy or by letting it be a market outcome. Or, to put it differently, *how* a certain level of NGDP is achieved is also important. Facing this issue, policy makers encounter what could be described as an application of Hayek's knowledge problem to central banking. In some instances, the market information required to correctly manage money supply is lacking given that the market process that takes place under free banking is not working anymore. Policy makers need to find a new variable to substitute for this information; this new variable will likely be less efficient in providing information than a pure market process. This means that policy makers need to be equipped with an above normal capacity to know what is going on in the economy. After the events seen in the 2008 financial crisis, it is not clear that this is a plausible assumption.

Chapter 6 discusses the 2008 financial crisis in the context of nominal income targeting and why the Federal Reserve reacted the way it did. This chapter does not offer a detailed "day-to-day" account of the crisis, rather it focuses on the larger picture and how some *unconventional* policy decisions made the crisis worse than it should have been if the Federal Reserve were targeting NGDP or a similar nominal income variable. A deviation from monetary equilibrium (Chapter 4) also explains why there was a housing bubble in the first place. This bubble, however, cannot be explained without taking into consideration regulation and the political behaviors in place in the years prior to the crisis.

Finally, Chapter 7 discusses some monetary reforms that would move our actual central banking framework toward nominal income targeting or monetary stability. The feasibility of returning to the gold standard, a long-standing topic, is one of these monetary reforms. But other less radical options are also included, such as a free banking reform based on fiat money, currency competition, and the development of an NGDP futures market. The intention of these reforms is to reduce the burden of how efficient a central bank's policy needs to be and let market forces, and new institutional incentives, contribute to spontaneously achieve monetary equilibrium.

Undoubtedly more research is needed in this area. The lack of policy-making experience on nominal income targeting, however, should not be a barrier to explore the benefits of considering how central banking, as long as it is a given institution, can be improved. Hopefully the effect of the pages that follow will be to trigger some interest in broadening the analytical approach to central banking.

1 Free banking and monetary equilibrium

Introduction

The evaluation of any monetary policy requires a benchmark that specifies what a central bank should achieve. Since central banks play a crucial role in the management of money supply, monetary equilibrium should be their main objective. Being in equilibrium means the same in the monetary market that it means in any other market; equilibrium is when the quantity supplied equals the quantity demanded. How to achieve this equilibrium, and how can we know that has been achieved – if we can know this at all – is a more difficult matter. In particular, what does monetary equilibrium look like? Interestingly, there seems to be no strict agreement in this important issue in the economic literature. As obvious as it may be what a central bank should achieve, how to achieve it and what it would look like is less clear. The predominant view of what an efficient monetary policy would look like points to consumer price level stability. But other points of view, like the one put forward in this book, suggest this does not need to be the case. Especially in the presence of productivity gains, monetary equilibrium occurs alongside a fall in the consumer price level (to be discussed in the next chapter).

The theory and history of free banking provides a depiction of what monetary equilibrium looks like and how it is achieved by the market without the aid of a central bank. A free banking system is a benchmark of what we should expect a *given* central bank to do and what its minimum level of efficiency should be. To justify the presence of a central bank, this institution should correctly aim for monetary equilibrium and outperform the market outcome. Otherwise, the market alternative – as imperfect as it may be – is a superior one. The topic of this chapter is to present an introduction to free banking and the market mechanisms in place that yield monetary equilibrium.[1]

What is free banking?

The first task is to define what constitutes a free-banking scenario. In particular, two misunderstandings in the critical literature of free banking should be avoided. Under free banking there is a free market in money *and* banking where the issuance of banknotes is supplied by private banks. What constitutes money can be

defined, like in most textbooks, as the asset with the three following characteristics present: (1) it is a common means of exchange, (2) it is a unit of account
(prices are denominated in units of this asset), and (3) it is a good store of value.

The first confusion to avoid is that free banking is not just the absence of a
central bank, but it is a market free of regulations and interventions. The financial
markets, however, can be heavily regulated by the government without need of
having a central bank. The distinctive aspect of a central bank is the monopolistic
power to issue money, not its regulatory powers. Countries without a central bank,
like Panama or Ecuador, do not have a free-banking scenario.

The second confusion to avoid is that free banking should not be understood
as the the perfect competition model where there is a large number of small producers of perfect substitutes. The idea of a market free of regulations should not
be interpreted in this sense, but as free – rather than perfect – competition, where
entry and exit is unhampered, and there is no regulation to protect or favor any
banks in particular. The fact that historical cases of free banking do not perfectly
resemble a perfect competition model neither implies that such cases are not historical instances of free banking nor that there is a kind of market failure under
free banking.

It is possible, at least in theory, to have different scenarios under a free market
of money and banking. Free banking is one of these potential scenarios (another
one, discussed in Chapter 7, is currency competition). Under free banking, outside
money (base money, high-powered money, or the ultimate means of payment) is
usually a commodity money, like gold or silver. It is assumed, for simplicity, that
economic agents hold their outside money as deposits in their bank accounts. Inside
money is composed of money substitutes in the form of convertible banknotes
issued by the private banks. Again, for simplicity, is assumed that banknotes are
the only money substitutes. In other words, outside money does not circulate from
hand to hand, inside money does. Each bank issues their own distinguishable
banknotes. Even though the terms outside and inside money have become quite
common in the recent literature, the old terminology of proper money (outside
money) and money substitutes (inside money) offer a better description of the
characteristics of each of this currencies (Mises, 1912, pp. 483–484). The reason
is that money substitutes, like convertible banknotes, substitute proper money, for
instance gold, in the day-to-day exchanges. Without proper money, there would be
no money substitutes, but there can be proper money without money substitutes.

While it is common to assume in free banking that outside money is a commodity like gold or silver, this does not need to necessarily be the case. It is possible to
imagine a free-banking situation where outside money is composed of fiat money
or newer developments like a digital currency (see Chapter 7). Note, however, that
under free banking, issuer banks do not choose what is going to perform as money
proper, this is a market outcome rather than a government decision. The reason
is that money substitutes (i.e. convertible banknotes) substitute proper money
(i.e. gold or silver), in the day-to-day exchanges. It is also possible to imagine
a free-banking scenario with two, or more, outside monies where private banks
issue convertible banknotes into either of them.

It is at least possible in theory to have a different monetary arrangement under a free market of money and banking. Currency competition *a la* Hayek is one of these possible scenarios (Hayek, 1976). In currency competition, private banks issue their own fiat currencies, rather than convertible banknotes into the same outside money. Note that under free banking, even if there is a large number of issuer banks, the unit of account remains unique based on whatever asset plays the role of outside money. There is no price confusion by a multiplicity of units of account. But in the case of currency competition, each bank issues a different fiat money, because if one bank prints gold and another one prints silver, in this case there is a multiplicity of units of account.[2]

More precisely, then, free banking is a particular outcome under a free market of money and banking. In particular, it is the setting historically observed in different countries in economic history. Alternatively, currency competition can be seen as a monetary reform proposal *given* the presence of central banks that aims to move the present monetary regime toward a more competitive market.

Monetary equilibrium in free banking

Money demand, money supply, and the price of money

Monetary equilibrium is the situation where the quantity of money supply equals the quantity of money demand. The quantity of money supplied is the amount of outside money plus the issued banknotes in circulation. Money supply can increase either because there is more gold being used as money or because banks issue more banknotes.

Money demand is the cash balance that economic agents want to keep liquid. It is the money that is not spent. The excess of money over its demand is spent in purchasing goods and services. Money used just to perform a transaction, then, is not money demand in the sense of holding a cash balance. Movements in money demand change the amount of money in circulation and therefore the price level (P).

Changes either in the money demand or money supply change the price of money or its purchasing power ($1/P$) just like change in demand or supply of any good would change the price of such market. This clarification would not be necessary without the widespread Keynesian view that interest rates, rather than the inverse of the price level, is the price of money. It should not be difficult to see that this is not the case. Consider the following example. An individual can lend 10 apples to another individual, who should return 11 apples a year after. This loan of apples has an interest rate of 10%. However, it would be hard to find anyone asserting that interest rate is the price of apples. For similar reasons, the idea that interest rate is the price of money should be rejected. The interest rate is the price of time (credit), not the price of the good used to make a time transaction. For pragmatic reasons, it is easier and more convenient to make a credit transaction with the most common accepted means of exchange, money. This, of course, does not make interest rate the price of money. As the apple example shows, interest rate is not even a monetary phenomenon; it is, in fact, a pure time phenomenon.

The confusion comes, in part, because central banks channel changes in money supply *through* the credit markets, which means that credit supply shifts at the same time central banks are expanding the supply of money. Central banks, however, could channel the increased money supply by buying apples. In this case, the price of apples will change rather than the interest rate. This would not make just the price of apples to be the price of money. Another way to see that the inverse of the price level is the price of money is to stand on the selling point of a transaction. The producer who sells apples for dollars is in fact buying dollars. From their point of view, the price is the inverse to the price seen by the consumer. Since money can be used to buy any good in the economy, its price is the inverse of the price level of all these goods.

Monetary equilibrium

In the case where money circulates only in specie (there are no money substitutes or convertible banknotes) if there is an increase in the demand for money, monetary equilibrium can only be achieved through a change in the quantity of specie (assuming money supply does not shift). The higher cost of extracting extra gold can be paid with the increase in the price of gold. In this case, the quantity of gold supplied needs to match shifts in money demand.

This is also one of the reasons why the gold standard is considered to be unstable. Unexpected (exogenous) discoveries of gold can result in price volatility and inflation. The same criticism applies to free banking, which can be seen as a gold standard without central banks. Not all gold discoveries, however, should be considered distortionary. Gold might be discovered (endogenous shift in supply) precisely because there was an increase in demand that asks for more gold in circulation as were the cases of South Africa (1874–1876), Colorado (1890s), and Alaska (1890s) (White, 1999, p. 38). While this instability of the gold standard is theoretically possible, it is not what is observed in history. Hogan and Smith (2015) show that during the 1792–1913 pre-Fed era, in the United States the two most significant increases of the price level occurred during the War of 1812 and the Civil War, not during famous gold discoveries. Another historical example of misplaced concern is the price revolution of the 15th century. During the price revolution, prices increased six-fold in Western Europe over a period of 150 years. This means the equivalent yearly inflation rate for this period was 1.30%, a low inflation rate for modern central bank standards.

When there are also convertible banknotes in circulation the situation is different. Money supply can now change by issuer banks changing the amount of banknotes in circulation. A shift in demand does not need to trigger a change in the quantity of money specie supplied; the shortage of money might be met with a change in the quantity of banknotes. This is, in fact, what is observed in free-banking episodes.

Individuals find it easier to use banknotes for commercial transactions than specie, and therefore they hold their money in the bank and carry the banknotes with them. Banks grant loans and issue banknotes such that they hold their desired level of reserve ratio.[3] If money demand increases, that means that purchases are decreasing and depositors' money balances increase. Therefore, banks see that reserves are now higher than their optimal level and in consequence issue more banknotes until the reserve ratio falls to the desired level again. The increase in money demand triggers, through the banks, an increase in money supply in the form of banknotes. If, on the contrary, money demand decreases, then purchases by consumers increase and bank balances decrease. Banks now see that the reserve ratio is too low and retire banknotes from circulation. A fall in money demand triggers, through the issuer banks, a fall in the quantity of money supplied as well. In this scenario there is no need to change the quantity of gold.

Through adverse clearing[4], changes in reserves also signal to banks if they are issuing too many banknotes. An issuer bank that puts into circulation more banknotes than individuals want to hold loses reserves through adverse clearing. Those banknotes that consumers hold in excess to their demand will be spent rather than hoarded, the expansionary bank will then lose reserves and the prudent bank will gain them. The cost of issuing banknotes for the bank is not only the cost of printing the banknotes, but also the increase in risk by reducing the reserve ratio to levels considered to be too low.

One advantage of free banking, where banks issue money substitutes, is that the money multiplier is independent of the banknotes/deposit ratio desired by the public. This is because gold is held in the banks rather than by the public. The banknotes that remain in the hands of the public do not affect the aggregate level of bank reserves. Let gold (B) be the base money, which in turn equals the stock of reserves (R); $B = R$. With fractional reserve banking, money supply (M) equals the amount of deposits (D) plus issued banknotes (N). If $r = \frac{B}{M}$ is the desired reserve ratio, then $\frac{1}{r} = \frac{D+N}{B}$. With B fixed, an increase (reduction) in banknotes held by the public increases (decreases) N and decreases (increases) D keeping $D + N$ constant.

In the case of a central bank that issues fiat currency the situation is different. In this case the public's desire of currency/deposit ratio does affect the money multiplier. This happens because all money is in the form of base money and there are no money substitutes in the form of claims against base money. The textbook money multiplier $\frac{M}{B} = \frac{1+c}{r+c}$ depends on the currency/deposit (c) ratio. This means that to keep monetary equilibrium, a change in c requires the central bank to adjust the supply of base money and deliver it to the banks. This base money adjustment when there is a change in the desired currency/deposit ratio is unnecessary under free banking. A decentralized market of money supply requires less information on the part of the issuer banks than the centralized scenario of modern central banks.

The larger the number of issuer banks, the higher cost bankers and depositors face in managing all the clearing transactions. It is also more costly to acquire information about the liquidity and solvency of each bank and whether or not a depositor or another bank should accept banknotes issued by an unknown bank. This information can be provided by private clearing houses (Dowd, 1990). For a bank to be accepted in the clearing house network it needs to comply with the financial requirements for membership. By being accepted in the clearing house network, a bank signals to the financial market that it is being efficiently managed by the clearing house standards. Banks only need to know if a bank is a member of the clearing house to accept their banknotes rather than study the financial situation of each one of them. The same type of information is provided to depositors when the clearing house certifies to the public that a given bank is a member of their network. The clearing house not only reduces the transaction costs of multiple clearings; it also works as a market certification process. Note that the clearing house neither has regulatory powers nor issues money. The clearing house is not analogous to a central bank in free banking (Dowd, 1994).

The absence of a central bank means that there is no lender of last resort in the way central banks play this role. But such absence does not mean lack of credit opportunities for banks. Indeed, each bank has, in principle, access to all banks that at least belong to the same clearing network if they are in need of liquidity. Also, the clearing house itself is an institution banks can turn to as a lender of last resort if other banks are not willing to lend to each other. Because the bank is a member of the clearing house, this institution has information about the financial situation of the bank asking for a loan. This means the clearing house is in a good position to differentiate between a bank that is insolvent and a bank that has a short-term liquidity issue but is solvent. Namely, the clearing house is in a position to sort out which banks should be issued a rescue loan and which ones should not. A market mechanism to distinguish between solvent and insolvent banks is to offer loans with a penalty premium in the interest rate. A bank that is illiquid but solvent would suffer a loss, but would not go bankrupt because of this loan. The self-interest of the members of a private clearing house goes against bailing out insolvent banks because the member would carry part of the losses of the insolvent bank if it goes bankrupt. But the same member can benefit from lending liquidity to an illiquid but solvent bank. This way, the clearing house contributes in keeping banking failures constrained to inefficiently managed institutions (more on bank runs and failures below). This is the principle behind Bagehot's rule. Bagehot (1873), who was not advocating a central bank, argued that *if* there is a central bank, it should lend to banks with a penalty premium as a mechanism to distinguish between banks that should be saved and banks that should not.[5]

Contractual and legal tools to avoid bank runs

It is well known that banks are short-run illiquid and prone to facing a bank run. Even though this is an issue of most economic activities because firms are unable to cancel all their debts and credit lines immediately, it is of special concern in banking (particularly in the absence of government deposit insurance). A market contract or legal tool designed to deal with this issue is the *option clause* or *notice of withdraw clause* attached to banknotes (Selgin and White, 1997). This was a common legal tool in the Scottish free banking before it was banned in 1765.

The main role of the option clause is to avoid a bank run on a solvent bank. Even though a bank may not be able to convert all the banknotes on the spot, it may have a non-liquid investment with enough market value to redeem all banknotes if enough time is given to cash its investment. With the option clause, the bank reserves the right to call in the option and redeem the value of the banknotes in no more than six months plus a two percent interest. This allows the banks to avoid a fire sale of their investments that could push the price of the financial assets down, worsening their solvency. The option clause would not stop a run on an insolvent bank, but it does avoid a self-fulfilling bankruptcy. It avoids, in short, the auto-prophecy where the claim that a bank would go bankrupt makes it so. In the case of Scotland's free-banking era, the inception of the option clause was not only to avoid potential runs on solvent banks, but also as a defense mechanism against note raids where a bank would collect a large amount of banknotes from a competitor and then try to convert them all at once as a way to harm the solvency of the competitor, a practice sometimes observed in the early stages of the Scottish free banking. The option clause, however, was rarely invoked by banks.

Another mechanism present in the Scottish case was the unlimited liability of the banks' shareholders (limited liability was not an option for non-chartered banks until 1862). Unlimited liability gives a very strong incentive to the shareholders, who were publicly listed, to efficiently manage the deposits signaling to the depositors that only good managers will be chosen by the bank owners. There were instances of bank failures, like the Ayr Bank in 1772 (see below), in which unlimited liability allowed depositors to save all of their deposits. Unlimited liability can also facilitate the acquisition of a failing bank by another institution, since part or all of the cost of covering the depositors' claims will be covered by the previous shareholders.

Alleged instabilities of free banking

Bank runs: micro versus macro

Because in free banking there is no financial regulation, no central bank, and therefore no official lender of last resort, the concern of sudden bank runs that could trigger a domino effect and put the financial system at risk plays an important role. If the public's concern about the financial solvency of the banks produces a bank run on solvent banks, then banks may be unable to secure loans from other banks because all financial institutions are in need of funds. A lender of last resort, in principle, can deal with issues like this one (also see the discussion in Salter (2016)).

Bank runs, however, should be distinguished between *micro* and *macro* bank runs. A *micro* bank run is when an insolvent bank loses its deposits and finally goes bankrupt. Note that this bank is insolvent *before* the bank run; it is its insolvency that triggers the bank run in the first place. The public, however, has not lost its confidence in the financial markets, but in a particular bank, or small group of banks. Given that the depositors have already manifested their preference to hold bank accounts, their run against the insolvent bank is done by transferring their accounts into other solvent banks rather than withdrawing their deposits from the financial markets all together. To assume otherwise implies changing the initial assumption about the preference for having deposits into bank accounts and changes the scenario from leaving an insolvent bank to leaving the financial system. What we observe in this case, then, is a re-allocation of deposits from poorly managed banks to more efficient banks. The market share of the banks changes and the solvency of the financial markets overall increases *because* some banks fail. This is no different from inefficient firms in other industries going bankrupt and more efficient firms gaining their market share.

Let us assume that it becomes public knowledge that a certain car manufacturer has produced a unit with a serious malfunction that could risk the safety of the driver and the passengers. This information could be disclosed by a firm that certifies the quality of the cars produced by their members (similar to the clearing house in free banking). In this case we expect consumers to change the brand of their car, but not to stop driving. This is a *micro* run against this particular car manufacturer. We can think of similar scenarios for other industries, for instance, if it is known that a certain food producer is producing goods that can make us ill. The public has reasons to change their financial services provider, but not to leave the financial service market. These bank runs do not put the financial markets at risk. An unlimited liability, or a private deposit insurance, can secure the deposits of the clients. It is also possible that the insolvent bank is bought by a solvent competitor securing the deposits of the insolvent bank.

A *macro* bank run occurs when the public loses its confidence not in a particular bank itself, but in the whole industry. This loss of confidence manifest itself initially as bank runs against certain banks because deposits are held at particular institutions, but not because the issue is with a particular financial institution. This is the case of systemic risk. This scenario is usually due to a problem that transcends a free-banking market. In a *macro* run not some, but all banks, managed by rational agents, become insolvent together at the same time. Historical instances of free banking certainly present *micro* bank runs, such as any industry goes through bankruptcies of some firms, but not of the whole industry. Selgin (1996, Chapter 9) shows that under free banking, bank runs were less frequent than under non-free banking regimes.

One possible explanation of a *macro* run is that economic agents become prisoners of irrational behavior (animal spirits). But it can also be the case that economic agents are observing wrong market information due, for instance, to regulation and interest rates movements by the monetary authority. This situation is usually produced by ill-designed financial regulation or economic policy. It can also be the case that a *macro* run is due to an increase in market uncertainty, for instance when government officials ask the public to not withdraw their deposits to avoid a financial crisis. This well-intended plea can produce the exact opposite effect.

The Diamond–Dybvig model

The Diamond and Dybvig (1983) model (DD model) is perhaps the main theoretical foundation of inherent instability in banking. This model is still used as a reference despite some important issues (Dowd, 1992a; Selgin, 1996, Chapter 11; White, 1999, Chapter 6). The mathematical consistency of this model is not under dispute, but its real-world relevance is. Mathematical and logical consistency does not imply that a model is either relevant or a good description of real-world economic phenomena.

In summary, the DD world works as follows. Assume that there is only one bank that represents the banking industry in a world of three periods $\{t = 0,1,2\}$. This DD bank issues neither loans nor checking accounts. Additionally, in this model there is no money and only one consumption good. Finally, there is no distinction between depositors and shareholders. Consider first the following situation. In period 0 all economic agents deposit a unit of the consumption good into the bank and receive in exchange a claim against this good. The bank invests the consumption good in a safe project that matures in period 2 at a rate of return $R > 1$. At the end of period 2 each depositor receives R. But, in period 1 each depositor discovers if he is Type-1 or Type-2. Type-1 depositors have a very high time preference because they will die in period 2; therefore, they want to consume in period 1. Type-2 depositors, on the contrary, have a low time preference because they expect to be alive in period 2. If the bank faces a withdrawal in period 1 it has to interrupt the production process. Since the consumption good deposited in the banks is undamaged, the depositor can recover their unit of good in period 1 without any gain or penalty. Imagine consumers deposit a unit of corn that the DD bank plants and harvests in period 2. If a depositor wants to withdraw a unit of corn, then the bank has to halt the production process in period 1; the unit of corn has not grown yet and the whole undamaged unit is delivered to the depositor.

In the DD world, however, any depositor could invest this consumption good by themselves. What the DD bank can offer is a way to pool risk through a different contract than the one discussed above. If r_1 and r_2 denote the returns of periods 1 and 2 respectively, then a contract that the DD bank can offer to depositors is one where the rate of returns are $R > r_1 > 1$ and $R > E[r_2] > r_1$. Namely, a depositor that wants to consume in period 1 can increase its consumption by making a deposit in the bank in period 0 and withdrawing in period 1. This means that the return in period 2 will be less than R because some consumption units that have not been claimed will have to be delivered. Also, because in period 0 the number of Type-1 and Type-2 depositors is unknown, r_2 is uncertain. What the DD bank is providing is actually an insurance against being a Type-1 depositor paid by the foregone return $(R - r_2)$ of Type-2 depositors. Type-2 depositors are willing to forego this return in exchange of the Type-1 insurance. The optimal value of r_2 depends on the expected proportion of Type-1 depositors. The DD bank is unstable, then, if in period 1 too many depositors call on their claims. This happens when Type-2 depositors are afraid there are too many Type-1 depositors and cause a run on the DD bank hoping to receive r_1 rather than 0 in period 2. In the case of a bank run, the DD model pays to the depositors on a first-come first-served basis. To avoid this potentially bad equilibrium, a government deposit insurance that eliminates the incentive to run against the bank is required.

The description of the DD model indicates that its connection to real-world banks is tenuous, at best. It is quite problematic to extend whatever merit is to be found in the inherent instability of a DD bank to real-world banking. As White (1999, pp. 128–129) points out, a first question that this model raises is how the banking industry survived centuries of competition if their contracts suffer from such inherent instability. The problem is that, by assuming only one DD bank, the model does not allow for a market competition discovery process that deals with this instability. In addition, by assuming only one bank, the DD model cannot distinguish between *micro* and *macro* runs, making of any bank run a systemic problem by construction. The case of a bank run against only inefficient banks has no place in this model. That means that an inefficient DD bank cannot lose market share through adverse clearing to the benefit of another efficient DD bank. This adverse clearing is at the core of banking competition in a free market of money and banking, but the DD model has no money and no adverse clearing mechanism.

There are different known market mechanisms that banks can use to deal with the problem raised by the DD model. One of them is the amount of equity they hold. In the DD model, the counterpart to assets consists of all liabilities. A DD bank has no equity, and therefore no cushion or resources to deal with a larger than expected withdrawal of deposits that would avoid an unnecessary bank run. By construction, the DD bank holds a zero-capital requirement. This capitalization is a tool that real-world banks have but the DD model lacks.

The absence of differentiation between depositors and shareholders means that unlimited liability, as discussed above, is not possible in the DD model. Unlimited liability can work as deposit insurance that also incentivizes share-holders to dispose of unstable contracts and inefficient managers. The presence of wealthy enough shareholders could also help avoid bank runs. Another alter-native is to assume the presence of economic agents with equity that provide a private insurance to the DD bank, rather than insurance being supplied by the government.

Another problem with the DD model is that it does not account for an option clause. In the DD world this would not be desirable since consumers deposit corn, and if a bank executes the option clause consumption is actually halted. Depos-itors would also starve if we take the corn analogy literally. This would not be an issue should the DD model account for the presence of money. A convert-ible banknote can still circulate and be used to buy consumption goods *even if* the issuer bank has executed the option clause and postponed convertibility. The Type-1 depositor with a high time preference can sell their banknotes (maybe at a discount) to a Type-2 depositor with a low time preference. Aggregate demand would not be affected and the bank run would have been avoided.

Finally, if a DD bank faces competition, another bank could offer a money-market mutual fund type of contract. In this contract, the depositor has a claim to a share of the mutual fund rather than a fixed nominal value. Therefore, if the value of the mutual fund drops, there is no incentive to run against the bank. In this case it is the depositors who are the ones bearing the cost and benefit of the risk in the value of the mutual fund. If the value falls, they bear the cost and the bank loses no equity. If the value rises, the depositors receive the gains, not the bank.

The DD bank is unstable by construction. Such construction, however, is not a fair representation of real-world banking, let alone free banking. Free banking should not be considered unstable due to the DD model outcome. Rather, historical records of free-banking performance are more illuminating.

Concerted expansion

The efficiency of adverse clearing as a mechanism to avoid an excess of money supply by the banks has traditionally been recognized to fail if banknote expansion takes place in-concert among all banks. When all banks increase the circulation of their banknotes in the same proportion, then all banks receive more banknotes from competing banks and the excess clearing across banks cancels out. In other words, the *expected* level of reserves remains unchanged in this scenario and, therefore, an excess of money supply becomes a possibility. A reason to question that such an in-concert expansion can take place is a similar reason to doubt that collusion is unstable due to entry of new competitors or a colluding firm deviating from the agreed strategy with its partners.[6]

This concern has been challenged, especially by Selgin (1996, Chapter 2; 2001) who builds on Baltensperger (1974). The argument is that even if, in the case of in-concert monetary expansion, the *expected* level of reserves remains unchanged for each bank, the *variance* of reserves does increase. As the *variance* of reserves increases, the likelihood of having less than the minimum level of reserves increases and this incentivizes the banks to halt their in-concert expansionary behavior.

The above argument can be shown formally. Following Baltensperger and Selgin, assume the bank wants to minimize the following cost (C) function by choosing the right level of reserves (R):

$$C = Ri + \int_R^\infty p \cdot (X - R) f(X) \cdot dX \qquad (1.1)$$

where i represents the interest rate at which the bank can issue a credit and p represents the cost of adjusting the level of reserves (to the desired level R); X is a random variable that tracks the net change in reserves with mean 0 and standard deviation $\sigma_X = \sqrt{PT}$ (PT represents the volume of transactions) and f(X) represents the probability density function of X. The first term represents the cost of opportunity of holding reserves and the second term represents the deviation cost from the desired level. The zero mean for variable X is consistent with a perfectly managed in-concert expansion. The normal distribution of this variable is also consistent with a large number of transactions.

Let $b = R/\sigma_X$ be the desired *coefficient of security* and $x = X/\sigma_X$ be the standardized X variable. Then (where f(x) represents the standard normal distribution):

$$C = b\sigma_X i + \sigma_X \int_b^\infty p \cdot (x - b) f(x) \cdot dx \qquad (1.1')$$

The banks minimize the cost function by choosing the optimal level of the coefficient of security (b^*), the first order condition yields the following result:

$$\frac{\partial C}{\partial b} = i - p \int_{b^*}^{\infty} f(x) \cdot dx = 0 \qquad (1.2)$$

This means that the desired level or reserves depends on b and also on the volume of transactions; $R^* = b^* \sigma_X = b^* \sqrt{PT}$. If the volume of transactions equals money supply (M) times its velocity of circulation (V_T), then: $R^* = b^* \sqrt{MV_T}$

This representation shows that the demand of precautionary reserves depends positively on the volume of transaction. But it also shows that unless money demand increases (making V_T fall), an increase in money supply also increases the level of precautionary reserves. Put differently, under monetary equilibrium, where money supply changes to offset changes in money velocity such that MV_T remains constant there is no need for the bank to adjust the demand of precautionary reserves.

A short note on the empirical evidence of free banking

While the above exposition is mostly theoretical, there are also a number of empirical studies of free-banking episodes.[7] Contrary to the prediction of models like the DD bank, historical episodes of free banking show that the system is endogenously stable. As V. C. Smith (1936) points out, central banks did not originate from the need of a lender of last resort and financial stability, but to finance fiscal deficits or, when related to financial instability, this was due to ill-designed regulation rather than a market failure like in the United States experience.

There are two points from the empirical literature on free-banking episodes worth pointing out. First, a closer look at alleged failures of free-banking episodes, in particular the United States and Argentina experiences, shows that such cases were not in fact free-banking instances. Second, how free banking deals with bank failures and government intervention can transform a *micro* run into a *macro* issue. This is illustrated by the cases of free banking in Scotland and Australia respectively.

United States and Argentina

It seems to be accepted that an unregulated money and banking market which results in crisis and financial instabilities is proven by the United States experience in the pre-Fed era (1873, 1884, 1893, 1907). This interpretation is captured by Rockoff's (1975, p. 160) description of this period as a natural experiment of laissez-faire banking. At first sight, the absence of a central bank and a number of private banks issuing banknotes seems to suggest that we are in the presence of a free-banking scenario. Absence of a central bank, however, does not mean we are in the presence of a free market of money and banking. Banking in the United States was far from unregulated in the pre-Fed era. Banking, for instance, was illegal unless a special permission was issued by the state government.

There are two particular regulations to take into account. The first one is that issuer banks were required to buy treasury bonds from their state as a way to secure their reserves. This produced a number of problems. In states with a poor fiscal situation, banks were required to secure their reserves with high-risk bonds. Regulation, not free market in banking, is what gave rise to the famous *wildcat (reckless) banking* by banks with the specific purpose of speculating with low-quality and highly discounted state bonds. Still, Dwyer (1996) argues that the issue of wildcat banking is exaggerated and without actual empirical support. This requirement to back the notes with government bonds also means that for money supply to react to changes in money demand, banks should be able to buy and sell state bonds when needed. But changes in the value stock of state bonds do not respond to monetary equilibrium requirements. During the Civil War the bond requirement was extended to federal debt. But after 1882 the federal government used fiscal surplus to reduce their outstanding debt, reducing the supply of bonds in the market. The rise in the price of the bonds made it harder for banks to acquire bonds and adjust money supply. The crises mentioned above occurred during the harvest season, when money demand increased but banks were unable to increase money supply.

The second regulation to consider is that banks were not allowed to open branches; which also meant that the state government could sell more charter permissions. This had a direct impact on risk diversification. A bank that opens for business in a town where the main economic activity is, say, growth of corn, is subject to cycles in this particular market. A season with bad weather can result in a banking crisis in this town. Banks were unable to diversify their portfolio both geographically and across different economic activities. Risk diversification is a key component of the business of banking. This restriction on the number of branches also made it harder and more costly to develop an efficient clearing system. This restriction incentivized the Suffolk Bank of Boston to start performing clearing services by itself between 1818 and 1858. Differently from an independent clearing house, the Suffolk Bank of Boston combined the roles of manager, owner, and member of the Suffolk club. However, the Suffolk Bank's experience is an exception, not the norm to be found in the pre-Fed banking era in the United States.

The United States pre-Fed banking stability can be compared with that of Canada. Unlike the United States, banks in Canada were allowed to open branches, diversify their risk, and move reserves geographically. Because Canadian banks were not tied to back their notes with treasury bonds, money supply was elastic enough to match cyclical movements in money demand (Selgin, 2010, p. 494). While during the Great Depression banks in the United States went bankrupt in the thousands, Canada saw no bank failures albeit also being significantly affected by the crisis (Laidler, 2005, n. 6). In addition, Canada did not have a central bank until 1935.

Similar confusion to that of the United States is present with respect to the Law of National Guaranteed Banks in Argentina between 1887 and 1890. This period is sometimes referred to as, or is implied to have been, a free-banking period in Argentina (Cortés Conde, 1989; Gerchunoff, Rocchi, and Rossi, 2008; Llach, 2007; Schuler, 1992). The confusion arises from the fact that there were several banks issuing their own convertible banknotes and on the fact that Argentina's government was inspired by United States free-banking laws. However, just like the United States' case, neither the absence of a central bank nor calling a legislation "free banking" means that there actually is a free-banking episode. The reason why the Argentine episode is relevant is because it triggered the Baring Crisis of 1890 and this invites the interpretation that this crisis was due to unregulated free banking. An important restriction was the restricted entry to the banking market, only five banks were allowed to issue guaranteed banknotes. Under the Law of National Guaranteed Banks, however, banks were an intermediary for the federal government that would issue external debt. The guaranteed banks were required to acquire treasury bonds in order to issue banknotes. The bank would borrow gold at the London Market and use the gold to buy treasury bonds from the Argentine government. In 1889 the Argentine government decided to pay the bonds with paper currency rather than gold, this implicit default triggered the Baring Crisis of 1890.

These two instances described as free-banking episodes show that a closer look at money and banking is required before concluding that monetary equilibrium is unachievable by the market itself. In particular, we should be cautious of not letting empirical findings confirm the outcome of models (i.e. DD bank) that, as formally consistent as they may be, fall short in depicting market phenomena as occurs in the real world.

Scotland and Australia

If the United States and Argentine episodes provide examples of what free banking is not, the episodes of Scotland and Australia provide insights into how free-banking actually worked. Surely there are no perfect episodes of free-banking. However, cases like those of Scotland and Australia provide good approximations in the sense that the institutional framework and incentives are similar to those of a free-banking arrangement. The fact, for instance, that basketball is played with some different rules in Argentina than in the United States does not mean Argentineans do not play basketball. The case is different if we want to evaluate the efficiency of basketball by observing the efficiency of baseball.

The Scottish free-banking era (1716–1844) is probably the most widely cited case. This free-banking episode also coincides with a significant development of the Scottish economy. The relation has not gone unnoticed. A. Smith (1776, bk. II.2), for instance, endorses the benefits of free banking and connects Scotland's economic performance to its money and banking institutions.

The free-banking episode in Scotland begins in 1716 when the Bank of Scotland (not a government bank), which was founded in 1695, let the monopoly privilege received upon foundation lapse giving freedom of entry to the banking sector. The Royal Bank of Scotland became the first competitor to the Bank of Scotland. In 1740 there were a total of five issuer banks, by 1769 the number of issuer banks were 32. Even without modern technology and the calculation power of modern computers, Munn (1981) figures show that once the clearing system was developed and functional the reserve ratio was as low as 2%.

A distinctive case is presented by Douglas, Heron, & Co. founded in 1769 in the town of Ayr, which came to be known as the Ayr Bank. The significance of the Ayr Bank comes from its bankruptcy three years later in 1772. This failure, rather than showing free-banking instability, shows the market's ability to separate inefficient from efficient banks. The Ayr Bank did not learn the lesson from the early years of free banking in Scotland and issued banknotes in excess. The Ayr Bank accumulated liabilities and resorted to credit from other banks to continue with its banknote expansion. The failure of the Ayr Bank also brought down another 13 small banks. The failure of these other banks was not because of a systemic risk or a bank run contagion, but because these 13 banks were over exposed by lending reserves to the insolvent Ayr Bank. The market discipline was constrained to the over issue by the Ayr Bank and to the other smaller banks that were financially supporting the Ayr Bank's strategy. More prudent banks remained in business. Competitors, like the Banks of Scotland opened new branches and new entrants joined the market within three years.

Competition and better management, rather than a lender of last resort, is what kept market confidence in the banking business. The day before the fall of the Ayr Bank, a number of competitors announced that they would accept Ayr banknotes. By attracting depositors the market shifts the market share (in terms of depositors and banknote circulation) away from the Ayr Bank toward more efficiently managed banks. The cost of accepting the Ayr banknotes was low for the other banks because of the unlimited liability discussed above. The 214 shareholders of the Ayr Bank paid in full the cost of the bank failure. The Ayr Bank failure depicts a case of a *micro* failure rather than a *macro* failure or systemic risk. It was the market competition itself that secured its own stability.

The free-banking episode came to an end in 1844 not because of its inherent instability, but due to Peel's Act and the subsequent Scottish Bank Act of 1845. By then there were 19 issuer banks still in operation. Banknotes from the Clydesdale Bank, the Bank of Scotland, and The Royal Bank of Scotland still circulate today.

The Ayr Bank shows how, under free banking, the market disciplines inefficient banks without falling into a systemic contagion. The crisis of 1890 during Australia's free-banking episode shows how government interference with the market process can make things worse. Also, like the case of Scotland, Australia's free-banking episode lasted for more than a century, starting in 1830 and ending in 1959. A strong development of the Australian banking market starts in 1835 with the foundation of the Australasian Bank. The development of the banking sector continued steadily until 1890, by then banks worked with a reserve ratio of around 4.5% (Dowd, 1992b, p. 57). In 1863 banks starts to gradually move to shareholders unlimited liability.

During the 1880s Australian banks issue credit to acquire real estate property. Toward the end of the 1880s, well managed banks perceived a potential reversion in real estate prices and started to reduce their risk exposure toward this market. But not-so-well managed banks continued to do business in the real estate market. The reversion of real estate prices was coupled by a worsening of the international exchange terms reducing the inflow of gold to Australia. In 1891 the Bank of Van Diemen's Land becomes the first one to fail. Banks that were dependent on the Van Diemen's took loans from the Federal Bank. If the Van Diemen's issued too many loans to the real estate market, the Federal Bank issued too many rediscount loans. By 1893 the Federal Bank could not face the withdrawals from a market that had lost its confidence in this bank. The Federal Bank was accepted, without much enthusiasm, into the Associated Banks network just three months before it declared the inconvertibility of its banknotes. The Associated Banks network was founded in 1892 with pressure from the government. When the Associated Banks decided to let the Federal Bank fail the uncertainty spread to the rest of the network members.

Another bank that was overexposed to the real estate market was the Commercial Bank. The government pressured the Associated Banks member to bailout the Commercial. Two of the largest members, the Union and the Australasia, were taking new depositors and were not inclined to bail out the Commercial at the expense of their solvency. Banks like the Union and the Australasia were gaining market share *during* the crisis, instead of being dragged down by the mismanagement of banks like the Van Diemen's, the Federal, and the Commercial. The failure of the Commercial Bank, however, triggered a government intervention that made things worse transforming a problem isolated to some banks into a *macro* banking issue. The government allowed the Commercial, in just four days, to open back to business with the same name but without the obligation of their previous liabilities. The efficiently managed banks, however, did not receive the government liability condonation. The situation changed and now depositors were transferring their bank accounts toward the Commercial. This resulted in an unnecessary series of convertibility suspensions and bank restructuring.

The second government interference with costly implications was a five-day banking holiday. The banking holiday, by forcing all banks to close their doors, increased the uncertainty in the eyes of the public. It is not as easy to sort out solvent banks (the ones that remain open) from insolvent banks (the ones that close their doors). The Australasian and the Union protested and tried to signal to the public that they were good for business. Under a forced bank holiday, however, the promise of solvency might not be as convincing as actually remaining open when other banks are closing their doors.

The crisis of 1890, during the Australian free-banking episode, shows how the banking failures were being compartmentalised by the market itself and it only became a systemic issue when the government decided to bail out banks like the Commercial. Setting aside the government intervention, then the failure of the Commercial might become the analogous case of the Ayr Bank failure in Scotland. The government intervention had yet another cost, which was the devaluation in the eyes of the public of a free-banking arrangement. The impression left in the public opinion was that of a market failure, not of a government failure. The demand for banking regulation increased and policy makers started to regulate the banking industry and bankers were presented as the source of exploitation and social injustice. After many years, including the international gold standard *de facto* suspension with World War I, Australia founded its central bank in 1959.

Notes

1 For a sample on the free-banking literature see Briones and Rockoff (2005), Cachanosky (2010), Dowd (1988; 1994), Dowd and Greenaway (1993), Hasan (1994), Sechrest (1993), Selgin (1988; 1996; 2001), Selgin and White (1988), V. C. Smith (1936), and White (1984; 2014).
2 On currency competition see Dowd and Greenaway (1993), Endres (2009), Fischer (1986), Friedman (1984), Luther (2013), Nash (2002), and White (1999, Chapter 12).
3 The reserve ratio is the proportion of deposits that a bank keeps as cash.
4 Adverse clearing is the net outflow of reserves from a bank that issues more convertible banknotes than the public wants to hold.
5 Consider this passage against central banking and in favor of free banking: "But it will be said–What would be better? What other system [than central banking] could there be? We are so accustomed to a system of banking, dependent for its cardinal function on a single bank, that we can hardly conceive of any other. But the *natural system–that which would have sprung up if government had let banking alone–is that of many banks of equal or not altogether unequal size.* In all other trades competition brings traders to a rough approximate equality. In cotton spinning, no single firm far and permanently outstrips the others. There is no tendency to a monarchy in the cotton world; *nor, where banking has been left free, is there any tendency to a monarchy in banking either.*" (pp. 66–67, emphasis added).
6 An example is Huerta de Soto (1998) who depicts the in-concert expansion scenario as a prisoner's dilemma. Huerta de Soto's scenario, however, shows a Pareto-optimal Nash equilibrium, rather than an sub-optimal equilibrium. See Cachanosky (2013).
7 Besides the literature in endnote 1, see Cachanosky (2012), Dowd (1992b), Dwyer (1996), Fink (2013), Hasan (1994), Laidler (2005), White (1984), and Zegarra (2013).

References

Bagehot, W. (1873). *Lombard Street: A Description of the Money Market.* London: Henry S. King & Co.

Baltensperger, E. (1974). The Precautionary Demand for Reserves. *American Economic Review,* 64.(1): 205–210.

Briones, I., and Rockoff, H. (2005). Do Economists Reach a Conclusion on Free-Banking Episodes? *Econ Journal Watch,* 2.(2): 279–324.

Cachanosky, N. (2010). The Endogenous Stability of Free Banking: Crisis as an Exogenous Phenomenon. *New Perspectives on Political Economy,* 6.(1): 31–48.

Cachanosky, N. (2012). The Law of National Guaranteed Banks in Argentina, 1887–1890: Free-Banking Failure or Regulatory Failure? *The Independent Review,* 16.(4): 569–590.

Cachanosky, N. (2013). Huerta de Soto's Concerted Expansion: A Prisoner's Dilemma in Free Banking? *Laissez-Faire,* 38–39.(Marzo-Septiembre): 1–6.

Cortés Conde, R. (1989). *Dinero, Deuda y Crisis.* Buenos Aires: Editorial Sudamericana.

Diamond, D. W., and Dybvig, P. H. (1983). Bank Runs, Deposit Insurance, and Liquidity. *The Journal of Political Economy,* 91.(3): 401–419.

Dowd, K. (1988). Automatic Stabilizing Mechanisms Under Free Banking. *Cato Journal,* 7.(3): 643–659.

Dowd, K. (1990). Did Central Banks Evolve Naturally? A Review Essay of Charles Goodhart's The Evolution of Central Banks. *Scottish Journal of Political Economy*, 37.(1): 96–104.

Dowd, K. (1992a). Models of Banking Instability: A Partial Review of the Literature. *Journal of Economic Surveys*, 2.(6): 107–132.

Dowd, K. (1992b). *The Experience of Free Banking*. London and New York: Routledge.

Dowd, K. (1994). Competitive Banking, Bankers' Clubs, and Bank Regulation. *Journal of Money, Credit and Banking*, 26.(2): 289–308.

Dowd, K., and Greenaway, D. (1993). Currency Competition, Network Externalities and Switching Costs: Towards an Alternative View of Optimum Currency Areas. *The Economic Journal*, 10.3(420): 1180–1189.

Dwyer, G. P. J. (1996). Wildcat Banking, Banking Panics, and Free Banking in the United States. *Economic Review*, Dec: 1–20.

Endres, A. M. (2009). Currency Competition: A Hayekian Perspective on International Monetary Integration. *Journal of Money, Credit and Banking*, 41.(6): 1251–1263.

Fink, A. (2013). Free banking as an evolving system: The case of Switzerland reconsidered. *The Review of Austrian Economics*, 27.(1): 57–69.

Fischer, S. (1986). Friedman versus Hayek on Private Money: Review Essay. *Journal of Monetary Economics*, 17.(3): 433–439.

Friedman, M. (1984). Currency Competition: A Skeptical View. In P. Salin (Ed.), *Currency Competition and Monetary Union* (pp. 42–46). Boston: Martinus Nijhoff Publishers.

Gerchunoff, P., Rocchi, F., and Rossi, G. (2008). *Desorden y Progreso*. Buenos Aires: Edhasa.

Hasan, I. (1994). Bank Runs in the Free Banking Period. *Journal of Money, Credit and Banking*, 26.(2): 271–288.

Hayek, F. A. (1976). *Denationalisation of Money* (2007 ed.). London: The Institute of Economic Affairs.

Hogan, T. L., and Smith, D. J. (2015). War, Money, & Economy: Economic Performance in the Fed and Pre-Fed Periods. *SSRN Electronic Journal*. http://dx.doi.org/10.2139/ssrn.2568634

Huerta de Soto, J. (1998). *Money, Bank Credit, and Economic Cycles* (2012 ed.). Auburn: The Ludwig von Mises Institute.

Laidler, D. (2005). Free Banking and the Bank of Canada. *Bank of Canada Review*, (Winter 2005–2006): 15–24.

Llach, L. (2007). *The Wealth of the Provinces: The Rise and Fall of the Interior in the Political Economy of Argentina, 1880–1910*. Doctoral Dissertation, Harvard University.

Luther, W. J. (2013). Friedman Versus Hayek on Private Outside Monies: New Evidence for the Debate. *Economic Affairs*, 33.(1): 127–135.

Mises, L. von. (1912). *The Theory of Money and Credit* (1981 ed.). Indianapolis: Liberty Fund.

Munn, C. (1981). *The Scottish Provincial Banking Companies 1747–1864*. Edinburgh: John Donald.

Nash, J. F. (2002). Ideal Money. *Southern Economic Journal*, 69.(1): 4–11.

Rockoff, H. (1975). Varieties of Banking and Regional Economic Development in the United States, 1840–1860. *The Journal of Economic History*, 35.(1): 160–181.

Salter, A. W. (2016). Robust Political Economy and the Lender of Last Resort. *Journal of Financial Services Research*, 50.(1): 1–27.

Schuler, K. (1992). The World History of Free Banking: An Overview. In K. Dowd (Ed.), *The Experience of Free Banking* (pp. 7–47). London and New York: Routledge.

Sechrest, L. J. (1993). *Free Banking. Theory, History, and a Laissez-Faire Model* (2008 ed.). Auburn: The Ludwig von Mises Institute.

Selgin, G. A. (1988). *The Theory of Free Banking*. Lanham: CATO Institute and Rowman & Littlefield.

Selgin, G. A. (1996). *Bank Deregulation and Monetary Order* (2002 ed.). New York: Routledge.

Selgin, G. A. (2001). In-Concert Overexpansion and the Precautionary Demand for Bank Reserves. *Journal of Money, Credit and Banking*, 33.(2): 294–300.

Selgin, G. A. (2010). Central Banks as Sources of Financial Instability. *The Independent Review*, 14.(4): 485–496.

Selgin, G. A., and White, L. H. (1988). Competitive Monies and the Suffolk Bank System: Comment. *Southern Economic Journal*, 55.(1): 215–219.

Selgin, G. A., and White, L. H. (1997). The Option Clause in Scottish Banking. *Journal of Money, Credit and Banking*, 29.(2): 270–273.

Smith, A. (1776). *An Inquiry into the Nature and Causes of the Wealth of Nations* (1979 ed.). Indianapolis: Liberty Classics.

Smith, V. C. (1936). *The Rationale of Central Banking and the Free Banking Alternative* (1990 ed.). Indianapolis: Liberty Fund.

White, L. H. (1984). *Free Banking in Britain. Theory, Experience and Debate, 1800–1845* (1995 ed.). London: The Institute of Economic Affairs.

White, L. H. (1999). *The Theory of Monetary Institutions*. Oxford: Basil Blackwell.

White, L. H. (2014). Free Banking in History and Theory. *GMU Working Paper in Economics No. 14–17*. Arlington: George Mason University.

Zegarra, L. F. (2013). Free-Banking and Financial Stability in Peru. *Quarterly Journal of Austrian Economics*, 16.(2): 187–226.

2 Nominal income targeting and the productivity norm

Introduction

Chapter 1 discussed how monetary equilibrium is achieved in the case of an unregulated market of money and banking. The finding of the free-banking literature is that money supply adjusts through market forces to changes in money demand. In particular, when there is an increase on money demand, money supply adjusts through an increase of convertible banknotes in circulation. This chapter takes a closer look at the conditions and characteristics of monetary equilibrium in a more formal setting. It is precisely the idea of monetary equilibrium that is behind the arguments in favor of nominal income targeting as a desirable monetary policy rule. A comparative analysis of different monetary rules is the subject of the next chapter; in this chapter, rather, the focus is on presenting an analytical framework of nominal income targeting in the context of two similar rules: (1) Hayek's rule and (2) NGDP Targeting.

The literature on nominal income usually refers to the quantity theory of money as its analytical framework and to differentiate real from nominal shocks. As long as we do not let slip from our minds that the quantity theory of money is a framework and, as such, imposes some analytical restrictions, it is indeed a useful way to represent monetary equilibrium in general and NGDP Targeting in particular. An outcome of particular interest is what Selgin (1996, Chapter 7) calls the *productivity norm*, which states that the price level should be allowed to change inversely in the presence of positive productivity gains. This outcome differentiates nominal income targeting rules from the popular approach of inflation targeting which aims at price level stability. Only under special conditions does price level stability result in monetary equilibrium, which means that this popular rule is biased with respect to its desired objective.

Monetary equilibrium and the equation of exchange

The quantity theory of money is typically used to state that money supply has a direct and proportional effect on the price level. In the analysis of nominal income targeting, however, the focus is primarily on monetary equilibrium (the left side of the equation), and not so much on the effects of money supply on the price level.

Therefore, attention to some details usually glossed over during the typical use of the quantity theory of money is needed. In order to have a better understanding of these details, it is useful to compare both the Cambridge and Fisher equations of exchange.

The Cambridge equation focuses on money demand (M^d), which is the share k of the nominal income ($P_Y Y$) that is held by the economic agents. In other words, it is the nominal income that is consumed as liquidity services rather than spent in acquiring goods and services (Horwitz, 1990; 2000, pt. II; Hutt, 1956). Equation 2.1 shows Cambridge's equation of exchange.

$$M^d = k \cdot (P_Y Y) \tag{2.1}$$

If the price level increases (decreases), then money demand increases (decreases) as well to keep the monetary real balance constant; a 5% increase (decrease) in P_Y results in a 5% increase (decrease) in M^d. Changes in real output (Y) give the same result. Share k, in turn, can be modeled as a variable that depends on transactions to be performed (i.e. a cash-in-advance – CIA – restriction), interest rates, liquidity preference (i.e. money-in-the-utility – MIU – function), etc. Note that if modeled this way, a change in these parameters would imply a shift in the demand for money, rather than a change in the price of money. In other words, a change in the interest rate can shift the demand for money, which is a different effect from the interest rate being the price of money (a movement *along* the demand for money).

Inversely, it could be said that Fisher's equation of exchange has its focus on money supply (M^s) rather than on money demand. Fisher's equation, however, does not look at output of final goods and services, it looks at *all* transactions (T) that occur in the economy. These transactions may or may not be associated with the acquisition of a new consumer good or service of inputs in the production process; these transactions also include financial transactions where a change of ownership takes place (i.e. buying and selling stocks). Equation 2.2 represents Fisher's equation of exchange.

$$M^S \cdot V_T = P_T \cdot T \tag{2.2}$$

where V_T and P_T are the money velocity of circulation and the price level associated with all transactions in the economy respectively. Because data for all transactions is usually not available, the focus of the empirical literature has been on real output transforming Equation 2.2 into Equation 2.3.

$$M^S \cdot V_Y = P_Y \cdot Y \tag{2.3}$$

If money supply equals money demand, then from Equations 2.1 and 2.3 it follows that $V_Y = \frac{1}{k}$. This means that money velocity can be interpreted as the inverse of money demand. A higher (lower) money demand implies a higher (lower) k and therefore a lower (higher) V_Y. If more (less) dollars are used to buy goods and services, then on average each dollar is circulating faster (slower).

A dollar parked in the wallet of an economic agent reduces the average "speed" of each dollar in the economy.

This merging of Equations 2.1 and 2.2 implies that the ratio $\frac{T}{Y}$ remains constant, which may or may not be the case in any given time period (Evans and Thorpe, 2013). While this assumption might be plausible for long-run effects such as the effect of money supply on the price level, which is the typical concern when using the quantity theory of money, this supposition is more questionable in the short-run where the focus is precisely on business cycles. This is also the particular problem to which nominal income targeting is applied. A more accurate theoretical use of the equation of exchange would focus on $P_T T$ rather than $P_Y Y$.

If the equilibrium condition ($M^d = M^s$) gives us Equation 2.3 where $V_Y = \frac{1}{k}$, then the free-banking scenario discussed in the previous chapter shows what the effects on the money market will be when there is a change in money demand. Assume a free-banking scenario where money proper (base money or high-power money) is gold (G) and let m be the money multiplier. Since M is composed of gold reserves *and* convertible banknotes, then Equation 2.3 can be opened up into Equation 2.4:

$$G \cdot m \cdot V_Y = P_Y \cdot Y \tag{2.4}$$

Two things happen when money demand increases. First, money velocity falls. Second, banks see their reserves increase above their desired level. This second effect signals to the banks that they should increase the circulation of banknotes until the reserve ratio falls again to its desired level. A fall in V_Y, then, is offset by a change in M. The increase in money supply can occur either by increasing G or by increasing m. As discussed in the previous chapter, an increase in money demand *does not need* an increase in gold under free banking. The inverse effects occur if money demand falls. When economic agents decrease the number of banknotes they hoard, banks see their reserve ratio fall below their desired level. This informs the banks that they need to withdraw banknotes from circulation. Then, an increase in V_Y is offset by a fall in M.

Monetary equilibrium, then, has two conditions, a *static* one and a *dynamic* one. The first one is the usual static requirement that quantity of money supplied equals quantity of money demanded. The dynamic one is that MV remains constant (more details on this condition below). If the objective of the monetary authority is to mimic the monetary equilibrium found in a free market of money and banking, then its objective should be to have M move proportionally and inversely adjust to changes in V_Y. In the context of the quantity theory of money, this is similar to keeping PY (NGDP) constant. It is this outcome that drives the nominal income targeting rules.

Nominal income targeting as monetary policy

In principle, a nominal income targeting rule can take different forms. It is not exactly the same, for instance, for Hayek's rule as for NGDP Targeting (discussed below). These two rules, in turn, are framed in the context of the equation of exchange as shown above. It is possible for a monetary rule with the objective of keeping monetary equilibrium to use target variables other than NGDP. For instance, a monetary authority may try to stabilize a proxy of P_TT, which will be more accurate since tracking all transactions is less accurate than looking only at the final ones. Or, as Niskanen (1992; 2001) suggests, the target variable could be final sales to domestic purchases (FSDP) instead of NGDP.[1]

A monetary rule needs (1) a *target variable* and (2) what *value* the target variable should have. These two components of a monetary rule are important decisions to be made by policy makers. But this is not a difficulty present only in a nominal income targeting rule. A similar problem is present in other rules such as an inflation target. In such a rule, policy makers need to decide what is the proper measure of inflation (based on CPI, core-CPI, GDP deflator, etc). and what is the right value for the chosen target. When different variables present a similar behavior, choosing the right target value is more important than choosing the right target variable. Since the behavior of NGDP and FSDP is similar, choosing the right target value becomes more pertinent than choosing between these two alternatives. Both, Hayek's rule and NGDP Targeting use NGDP as their target variable, but they differ on what the target value should be.

Hayek's rule[2]

Hayek (1931, p. 124) explicitly says that for money to remain neutral toward prices, money supply should compensate changes in money velocity (money demand). Hayek (1937, pp. 83–84) repeats his position stating that a central bank should offset changes in money demand by changing the supply of liquid assets (i.e. money). In terms of the equation of exchange, what Hayek is arguing is that MV should remain constant, rather than setting a path just for M or to stabilize P. Hayek's rule, then, consist in keeping MV constant (in per capita terms).

Hayek's concern is that, since changes in money supply are channeled through the credit market, an increase in M without a fall in V would reduce the interest rate below its natural or equilibrium level. Since interest rate is the price of time, time allocation in the production process will be distorted at the microeconomic level resulting in what is usually referred as the Austrian Business Cycle Theory (ABCT).[3] Hayek's rule implies that M should neither increase nor fall unless V is moving in the opposite direction.

A few clarifications are needed. The first one is Hayek's use of *money neutrality*. Hayek (1931) is not arguing that changes in money are neutral but, on the contrary, because changes in money supply *do* affect prices and interest rates (at least in the short-run), the *right* monetary policy should be put in place to avoid market distortions. Hayek's rule is neutral in the sense that does not produce distortions in the relative prices and therefore minimizes the noise in the information provided by market prices. If money demand does not change and money supply either increases (decreases), then a surplus (shortage) disequilibrium in the money market will have non-neutral effects in the economy.

Second, Hayek's position (and by implication those of the "Austrian" econo-mists) has been described as liquidationism (DeLong, 1990; 1998). Such a view of Hayek and the Austrians is still common today. The liquidationist policy refers to the behavior of the Treasury and the Federal Reserve of the United States in the early 1930s. The liquidationist position would let spending behave pro-cyclical as much as necessary to produce what would be a fresh start in the economy right after a crisis. A sound economic recovery requires, the argument goes, that all previous mistaken resource allocations are *liquidated* as fast as possible. The resemblance to Hayek's position and the ABCT, where the bust is the cost of errors accumulated during the boom, is patent. In addition, Hayek's alleged liquidationism finds an echo in Rothbard's (1963, p. 21) statement that after a crisis deflation, helps to speed up the recovery and that therefore the government should let the credit contrac-tion happen and *do not* interfere in the adjustment process. Rothbard's words can be interpreted as that of a liquidationist where "do not interfere" means freezing money supply even when money velocity falls. Yet, even if Rothbard's position is a liquidationist one, Rothbard's position does not make Hayek and the rest of the Austrians liquidationists as well. Differences among "Austrian economists" exist just as they do in any academic school of thought.

Contrary to DeLong, White (2008) shows that there are several issues with the liquidationist interpretation of Hayek. It should be clear now that Hayek's rule does not call for a freeze of money supply in the midst of a crisis because his rule explicitly calls for adjustment of M when money demand increases. It would be just as mistaken to associate nominal income targeting with a liquidationist position (as defined here) because under some conditions it allows the price level of final goods to fall, as it would be mistaken to describe Hayek as a monetary interven-tionist because he recommends money supply to increase under certain particular conditions. If money demand increases due to uncertainty on part of consumers and investors, then Hayek's rule calls for a reciprocal increase in money supply. This is not liquidationism. What Hayek's rule does not call for is for an increase in money supply that goes *beyond* the increase in money demand as a way to stim-ulate the economy. To produce a monetary disequilibrium by increasing money supply more than the increase in money demand cannot, in Hayek's view, cure a depression. Another issue with the liquidationist reading of Hayek is that his point of view on business cycles was unknown to the English-speaking world until his *Prices and Production* was published in 1931 in the United Kingdom; too late to have a significant influence, if any, in the early 1930s economic policy debate in the United States. White (2008) shows that rather than Hayek's thoughts, the Federal Reserve was influenced by the *real bills doctrine*, which states that money supply should change with the level of economic activity.[4] Furthermore, Hayek (1931, p. 105) explicitly rejects the notion that the quantity of money supply should vary when production increases or decreases in the opening of Lecture IV.[5]

Finally, the term "Hayek's rule" should not be understood as Hayek being a loner in stating that a central bank should stabilize MV. That a central bank should offset changes in money demand was a position held by well-regarded economists of the time such as D. Davidson, A. Marshall, N. G. Pierson, F. Edgeworth, F. W.

Taussig, L. von Mises, A. C. Pigou, E. Hicksher, B. Ohlin, G. Myrdal, and G. Haberler among others (Selgin, 1996, Chapter 8). Until the Keynesian revolution shifted the emphasis from relative prices to economic aggregates, a principle as the one behind Hayek's rule was not an uncommon position to find among economists concerned with issues of monetary policy.

NGDP Targeting

NGDP Targeting has a similar structure to Hayek's rule. The main difference is not so much in the *structure* of the rule, but in the chosen target. NGDP Targeting, associated with the *Market Monetarists*, gained popularity after the subprime crisis. Of course, other studies on NGDP Targeting, even prior to the subprime crisis, can also be found.[6]

According to Christensen (2011) and Sumner (2012), NGDP Targeting implies, first, targeting the level or path of NGDP and, second, keeping a constant growth rate of NGDP. Because of the first condition this rule is also referred as NGDP Level Targeting. Targeting the path or level means that upward or downward deviations from the NGDP trend should be corrected as soon as possible by the monetary authority. The reason for this is that the market expectations regarding the nominal income would probably not have changed and therefore a reversion back to its pre-crisis level would be less costly than having the agents realize that their expectations are proven wrong. If NGDP falls (rises), then, the central banks should quickly bring NGDP, or MV, back to its original level to avoid a liquidity shortage (excess). The growth rate of the NGDP Target rule may vary from author to author, but Sumner's 5% yearly growth rate can probably be regarded as the main reference. Where this 5% is coming from and why it is the right target is less clear though. It seems to originate from observing the NGDP growth rate on the years prior to 2008, when it can be argued that implicitly the Federal Reserve was targeting a constant 5% growth rate of NGDP (Sumner, 2012, p. 12). This scenario, however, also accepts the interpretation that the 5% growth rate of NGDP was because of a too loose monetary policy rather than being the right NGDP target. In other words, the fact that the economy looked good *before* the 2008 financial crisis does not mean that the economy was, in fact, in good condition. Surely, an economy in a good condition will produce good economic indicators, but it cannot be inferred from observing good economic indicators that the economy is in a good condition. The observed 5% growth rate of NGDP on the years prior to the 2008 financial crisis is not itself a proof that such a number is a good (or bad) target. The same observed growth rate of NGDP can be used to argue that the excess of money supply ($\Delta M > \Delta V$) is what produced the housing bubble in the first place (discussed in Chapter 6). It could also be argued that the growth rate of NGDP should be always the same regardless of its value, what matters is to not add volatility to changes in nominal income to avoid differences between nominal income expectations and the actual nominal income received. It happens to be that NGDP was growing at a steady 5% in the years prior to the 2008 crisis.

Similar to Hayek's rule, NGDP Targeting aims to stabilize aggregate demand. In the case of Hayek's rule, the target implies a fixed aggregate demand, while in the NGDP Targeting version aggregate demand grows at a constant rate. Both rules would move NGDP back to its level if there is a significant deviation from its historical path. While Hayek does not present his policy recommendation in the form of a rule, and therefore some details like targeting the NGDP level are not clearly laid out, his call for *stabilizing* nominal income where movements in M offset movements in V implies a level target as well. In the particular case where population grows at 5% a year, then NGDP Targeting would be equal to Hayek's rule, where population is implicitly assumed to be constant.

From a policy-making, pragmatic point of view, adopting NGDP Targeting allows targeting of unemployment and inflation at the same time. If, for instance, the desired inflation target is 2%, then the MV growth rate target should be the long-run or trend growth rate of real GDP plus 2% inflation. In dynamic form, this rule will look as Equation 2.5.[7]

$$\dot{M} + \dot{V}_Y = \pi^* + \dot{Y}_{LR} \tag{2.5}$$

where the dot denotes growth rates, π^* is the target inflation, and Y_{LR} is the long-run or real GDP trend. While Hayek's rule implicitly targets at a zero rate of inflation, NGDP Targeting favors a positive rate of inflation. For a dual mandate like that of the U.S. Federal Reserve, this setting implicitly targets both mandates at the same time. When the economy decelerates (accelerates) and unemployment rises (falls), then the price level increases (decreases) without the need for short-run discretionary behavior on the part of policy makers. Also, this framework constrains the policy makers' ability to increase the price level for a short-run benefit (i.e. exploit the Phillip's Curve relationship). Furthermore, in this framework the correct change in the price level does not need to be estimated because it is an outcome of the rule. In other words, policy makers do not need to answer the question of "how much inflation is necessary with this level of unemployment?" Then, targeting NGDP, or MV, does not require for policy makers to specifically know how to target the real growth rate and inflation separately. Rather, policy makers need to focus on keeping monetary equilibrium.

As a final point, we can move from the equation of exchange to a rule formula by adding a term to adjust for level changes in NGDP as shown in Equation 2.6.

$$MV_t = NGDP_t + \lambda(NGDP_{t-1} - NGDP^*_{t-1}) \tag{2.6}$$

where the subscript t denotes the time period, $NGDP^*$ is the desired level of $NGDP$ and λ has value between 0 and 1. If $\lambda = 0$ then the NGDP rule does not correct for level deviations, and if $\lambda = 1$ then the level deviation should be corrected entirely in the current period. What this formula shows is how much of the deviation from the desired target is added or subtracted from the current period's NGDP.

Nominal income targeting and productivity shocks

The most salient feature of nominal income targeting, in comparison to a price level stability policy such as inflation targeting, is that the former is able to distinguish between nominal shocks and real shocks. The distinction between the two rules comes from the fact that only on special conditions does a stable price level (zero inflation rate) equal monetary equilibrium. From the money market equilibrium condition $M \cdot V_Y = P_Y \cdot Y$ where MV_Y is constant, it follows that $P = \frac{MV_Y}{Y}$. Since monetary equilibrium implies that MV_Y is constant, then the price level should be allowed to change inversely with changes in real output. Stabilizing the price level is not the same as targeting monetary equilibrium.

The prescription for the behavior of the price level in nominal income targeting rules contrasts with that of an inflation targeting rule. In the presence of productivity gains, an inflation target rule calls for an expansion of money supply, but because money demand has not increased, the result is to produce an excess of money supply in the money market. Selgin (1996, Chapter 7; 1997, Chapter 2) refers to the price level changing proportionally and inversely to changes in productivity as the *productivity norm*. The distinction between nominal and real shocks allows separation between good (benign) and bad (malign) deflation. Good deflation is the result of productivity gains or, in the aggregate demand and aggregate supply framework (AD-AS), a shift to the right of the long-run aggregate supply. The idea that deflation is always a bad economic symptom is so widespread, that a fall in the vertical-axis (price level) is interpreted as a left movement on the horizontal-axis (output) of the AD-AS model. A bad economic situation such as a depression, however, is captured by horizontal movements in the AD-AS model, not by vertical movements in the price level axis. A central bank committed to inflation targeting that wants to avoid producing monetary disequilibria needs to be discretionary and explicitly distinguish what type of shock is driving a change in the price level at each point in time: a nominal one or a real one. Under nominal income targeting, policy makers neither need to be discretionary nor need to know when to stabilize the price level.

It is difficult to find historical instances of good deflation after the Keynesian revolution emphasis on price level stability. But such episodes are not unknown in economic history if we expand our historical range to include the years prior to Keynes and the appearance of central banks. An example of such episodes is the Great Depression of 1873–1896 in the United Kingdom. Giffen (1904, pp. 108–109) argues that a close inspection of data shows the opposite picture to that of a depression. Certainly some particular industries might have gone through hard times, but at the aggregate level the crisis does not show up. Giffen (1904, p. 176) shows that taxable income increased during the depression era rather than fell. Aggregate supply was moving to the right (increasing) rather than to the left (decreasing). Similar results are shown by Friedman and Schwartz (1982, table 4.9).[8] In addition, Atkenson and Kehoe (2004) find little empirical link between deflation and depressions in a sample of seventeen countries and a 100-year time period. These authors find *more* instances of deflation *with* growth than of deflation with depression, and more cases of depression with inflation than of depression with deflation.

We can expand this analysis to show how changes in real output can affect money demand. Let Y be a Hicks-neutral or factor augmenting production function and let money demand be a function of population and real income. Then Equation 2.3 becomes Equation 2.7.

$$M \cdot V_Y \left(L, \frac{Y}{P_Y} \right) = P_Y \cdot A \cdot F(K, L) \tag{2.7}$$

where A is total factor productivity (TFP), F is a production function (i.e. a Cobb–Douglas production function), K is capital, and L is labor. In this representation money demand is also a function of labor (population) and real income. The term "productivity norm" is meant to capture increases in Y. Output can increase either because of higher productivity or a larger endowment of factors of production. In either case, the monetary authority should keep MV constant.[9] The implications of this can be shown by assuming a Cobb–Douglas production function as shown in Equation 2.8 (where $0 < \alpha < 1$).[10]

$$M \cdot V_Y \left(L, \frac{Y}{P_Y} \right) = P_Y \cdot A \cdot K^\alpha \cdot L^{1-\alpha} \tag{2.8}$$

The log differential of Equation 2.8 yields the growth rates (denoted with dots) shown in Equation 2.9 (recall that $\pi_Y = \dot{P}_Y$).

$$\dot{M} + \dot{V}_Y = \pi_Y + \dot{A} + \alpha \dot{K} + (1-\alpha)\dot{L} \tag{2.9}$$

Since $\dot{M} + \dot{V}_Y = 0$ it follows that under monetary equilibrium, the change in the price level can be represented by Equation 2.10.

$$\pi_Y = -\dot{A} - \alpha \dot{K} - (1-\alpha)\dot{L} \tag{2.10}$$

If the endowment of the factors of production is fixed $(\dot{K} = \dot{L} = 0)$, then the price level moves inversely and in the same proportion as changes in productivity $(\dot{A})$. But from Equation 2.10 it also follows that the price level is expected to move inversely to changes in the endowment of factors of production according to their respective marginal outputs. Since money supply will offset any change in money demand due to an increase in a factor of production, such as labor, the price level would still move inversely to changes in output.

In addition, since nominal income also equals the income of the factors of production, Equation 2.8 can also be written as Equation 2.11

$$M \cdot V_Y = p_L \cdot L + p_K \cdot K \tag{2.11}$$

Applying the log differential to Equation 2.11 and assuming that labor and capital endowments are fixed ($\dot{L} = \dot{K} = 0$), we get Equation 2.12

$$\dot{M} + \dot{V}_Y = \dot{p}_L \cdot L + \dot{p}_K \cdot K \tag{2.12}$$

It follows from this expression that monetary equilibrium implies stabilizing an index of nominal income of the factors of production (P_{FP}) such as $P_{FP} = p_L \cdot \omega_L + p_K \cdot \omega_K$, where $\omega_L = \frac{L}{K+L}$, $\omega_K = 1 - \omega_L$. Since $\dot{M} + \dot{V} = 0$, it also follows that $\dot{p}_L = -\dot{p}_K \left(\frac{K}{L}\right) \rightarrow \dot{P}_{FP} = 0$.

As explained at the beginning of the chapter, a more accurate monetary equilibrium representation implies taking into account not just the production of final goods and services, but all transactions performed in the economy (Equation 2.2). Since Equation 2.11 implies all transactions in the economy, it follows then, that to target NGDP is an approximation and an indirect way to stabilize the nominal income of the factors of production.

Equation 2.7 also shows that money velocity may not be independent from supply shocks, and therefore money supply would also be affected by supply shocks. Money velocity can change, first, if the increase in output results in an increase in labor supply. If labor supply is elastic to changes in income, then the increase in labor increases the aggregate demand of money and therefore money velocity falls. Monetary equilibrium calls for an increase in money supply to keep MV constant. Second, money demand can change when real income increases. If a rise in real income results in a fall in money velocity, then M should increase to keep MV constant.

The *productivity norm* points to an important and forgotten lesson, neither inflation nor deflation *per se* are bad for the economy. When deflation (inflation) is the result of a money shortage (surplus), deflation (inflation) is then the outcome of a monetary disequilibrium and as such adds costs and welfare loss to the economy. But when deflation (inflation) is the result of an increase (decrease) in output, then this is a benign situation. The two scenarios are fundamentally different; a right (left) shift in aggregate supply is not the same as a left (right) shift in aggregate demand. An increase in output changes the proportion of money to goods and, therefore, the price of money is expected to increase, which is captured by a fall in P which produces an increase in the price of money $\left(\frac{1}{P}\right)$. In other words, benign inflation and deflation are a relative price change, while malign deflation and inflation is the result of market disequilibrium.

The discussion in this section invites revision of three issues. The first one is what is to be understood as inflation if there is more than one reason why the price level can change. The second one regards what is the cost of adjusting prices of final goods downward when money demand increases but money supply remains constant. And the third one is the effects of benign deflation on wealth redistribution.

Redefining inflation

Inflation is typically defined as a persistent increase in the general price level of final goods and services. Historically, however, inflation was understood as an excess of money supply over money demand. In a simple scenario, such as a closed economy where, *ceteris paribus*, there is an increase in money supply, it is to be expected that there will be an increase in the price level of final goods. If this is the case, then it is feasible to measure inflation by comparing the price level in any period *t* with the same price level in a previous period. But an issue that remains, even in this simple scenario, is that *if* there is more than one reason why the price level may change, then defining inflation by describing a movement of a variable that can have multiple reasons invites confusion. This confusion can eventually lead to errors in monetary policy. More accurate would be to define inflation by its *cause* rather than its effect.

The real world is more complex than the above simple scenario and it is possible that this way to measure inflation (comparing the price level across time) conceals a monetary disequilibrium behind a stable price level. One reason this situation may happen is that an excess of money supply is spent on goods that are not included in the CPI or in the GDP deflator (this issue will be important in Chapters 5 and 6).[11] Another reason for a monetary disequilibrium and a stable price level to occur simultaneously is when the upward effect (on the price level) of an excess of money supply is offset by the downward effect of productivity gains.

If the idea of inflation as an increase in the price level of final goods and services is driven by the idea that this is caused by an excess of money supply, then an ideal measurement of inflation that focuses on the price level should compare the actual price level with what the price level *should have been absent the excess of money supply*. Because the latter is not observable, in practice price levels are compared across time. Let us assume that due to an excess of money supply the price level should increase 5%, but because of productivity gains the price level would fall 3%. By comparing the price level across time what we see is an increase of 2%. The price level, however, *should have* fallen by 3%. Total inflation, 5%, can be divided into an *explicit* inflation of 2% and an *implicit* inflation of 3%. Inflation, however, is defined as a change in the price level that is measured in a way that ignores the presence of productivity gains or implied inflation. If this implied inflation is ignored, or considered unimportant, then the monetary authority can underestimate the real level of inflation in the economy. Like an iceberg, in the presence of productivity gains only a part of total inflation is observed as an increase in the price level.

It might seem that this section is more concerned with semantics than anything else. However, to the extent that this is the case, these semantics matter. If inflation is to be defined as a change in the price level rather than as an excess of money supply over money demand, then monetary authorities should bear in mind that *not* all changes in the price level are of the *malign* type. A central bank should not always be afraid of deflation (a positive productivity shock) and should not always try to control inflation (a negative productivity shock). Since the definition (semantics) of measuring inflation as a change in the price level of final goods does not equal monetary equilibrium, the focus on price level stability can set the monetary authority off-track. As a word, inflation is attached to negative connotations, but as a phenomena, inflation defined as a change in the price level can have multiple causes, but not all of these causes are bad. To the extent that semantics have an influence on monetary policy (even if indirectly through the public opinion), then semantics do matter.

If the monetary authority wants to stabilize the price level, it will need to increase money supply in the presence of productivity gains. Otherwise it will face deflation, a word with a worse negative connotation than inflation. But the issue is that this price level stabilization policy does not make inflation disappear; it translates it from the price level of final goods to the price level of intermediate goods. In the presence of productivity gains, then, either the price of final goods or the price of intermediate goods will have to adjust. It is not so much an issue of whether or not there will be inflation or deflation as it is an issue of which price level will capture this effect. The next section considers why letting the price of final goods fall is less costly than letting the price of intermediate goods rise.

Menu costs

In the presence of a productivity shock, the price level of final goods will fall if the monetary authority is following a nominal income target rather than an inflation target. But if the monetary authority follows an inflation target, then the price level of intermediate goods and factors of production will rise. This raises the question of which price level, that of final goods or of intermediate goods, has a less costly adjustment. Selgin (1996, pp. 150–156; 1997, pp. 25–29) presents this in terms of menu costs by looking at the number of prices that would have to change in either case. Assume there are n final goods and f factors of production. Assume also that the cost of adjusting any of these prices is the same. We can now develop three scenarios.

In the first scenario there is a productivity shock that affects the production of only one final good, then only one price would fall. However, if the monetary authority policy is to keep the price level of the n consumer goods (CPI) stable, the monetary authority needs to increase money supply until $n-1$ prices have increased such that CPI remains constant. This scenario resembles the fall in prices in the last decades of electronic goods such as personal computers and mobile phones. This industry grew significantly despite seeing the price of their goods fall consistently and it would hardly be described as a deflationary situation for the economy or its own industry.

In the second scenario the productivity shock affects all but one final good, then in the case of a monetary equilibrium policy, $n-1$ prices will adjust downward; and in the case of price level stability, $n-1+f$ prices will have to adjust. Since the productivity shock significantly affects the economy, CPI cannot be stabilized without affecting FPI (factor of production price index). But if the monetary authority keeps MV stable, then only f prices will have to change. As long as the productivity shock affects all but one consumption good, a monetary equilibrium policy requires fewer prices to adjust than a zero inflation policy.

In the third scenario the productivity shock affects all n final goods. This is the scenario where it is theoretically possible for a zero inflation policy to require less price adjustments than a nominal income target policy. For a zero inflation or stable price policy to require fewer prices to adjust than a monetary equilibrium policy two conditions needs to be present. First, that the productivity shock affects all *n* goods *and* that there are less factors of production than final goods. Both conditions, however, are not very plausible. Productivity gains occur in specific economic sectors at different points in time and larger productivity gains affect different industries at different points in time. Second, while for mathematical convenience factors production is usually aggregated into just two variables in economic models (capital and labor), the production of each *n* goods requires a large number of heterogeneous capital goods and heterogeneous labor specialization. The scenario where a productivity shock affects all *n* goods at the same time and $f < n$ is theoretically possible, but quite unlikely. If the monetary authority wants to keep monetary equilibrium and minimize the number of prices that need to adjust when productivity gains happen, it will be on safer ground by following a nominal income target policy than a zero inflation policy.

It could be argued, however, that in scenarios 1 and 2 there will be a second round of price effects following the productivity shocks and that, therefore, the prices of the factors of production will also change. The change in the relative price of the factors of production, however, is an outcome of a change in the relative price of the final goods due to the industry-specific productivity gains. This change will be present regardless of what happens to the price levels. Since this effect is present in both scenarios, it does not affect the result discussed above.

Further, without questioning here the assumption of money neutrality, a zero inflation policy also adds noise to the relative prices through a Cantillon Effect (see Chapter 4). In the case of industry-specific productivity gains, price adjustments occur more directly than under a zero inflation policy. This is because productivity gains are usually the result of an aimed entrepreneurial strategy or decision. But an increase in money supply to offset a benign deflation affects different sectors at different points in time. Since money supply enters the market through a specific point, some demand schedules are affected before others. The first consumer to receive newly printed money can increase their spending before the price level has increased. But, for the last consumer prices rise before they receive their share of newly created money. Therefore, demand lines for different consumer goods move at different points in time. The monetary authority cannot guarantee that money supply will reach the right industries at the right time. This Cantillon Effect implies an extra cost to the price adjustment under a zero inflation policy in the presence of productivity gains.

Wealth redistribution

Since in the case of a monetary equilibrium policy such as nominal income targeting the price level of final goods changes inversely to productivity gains, the real cost between a debtor (D) and a creditor (C) involved in a loan with a fixed interest rate payment might be affected. Two objections, then, can be put against a nominal income target that allows the price level to change. The first one is that, since fixed nominal debts are quite common in the economy, to let the price level change adds risk to debt contracts which in turn makes more long-term contracts relatively more risky. The second objection is an ethical one and questions why the debtor or creditor should be allowed to benefit from an unexpected change in the price level.

This wealth transfer between debtors and creditors can be captured with Fisher's equation: $i = r + \pi^e$; where i is the nominal interest rate, r is the real interest rate, and π^e is the expected inflation. If when the maturity of the contract arrives, real inflation (π) is different from expected inflation, then there is a wealth transfer between debtors and creditors. If inflation is larger than the expected inflation, then the debtor wins at the expense of the creditor, and the opposite occurs if inflation is less than the expected inflation. This case of wealth transfer, however, assumes that changes in the price level occur because of movements in the aggregate demand (AD), not by movements in the aggregate supply (AS).

If the difference between the expected inflation and real inflation is due to movements in AD, then it is the case that the debtor or the creditor benefits at the expense of the other. But the case of a price level movement due to a change in AS (productivity) is different because in this scenario real income *also* changes. And in this case the effects of the price level on the fixed debt contract and on real income are opposite to each other.

If the price level falls due to an increase in output, then the debtor is facing a higher cost on its debt to the creditor because the agreed nominal payment is fixed, but his real income has increased as well. Note that in this case, because AD has not changed, the nominal income of debtors *has not* fallen. It is not the case anymore that an unexpected fall in the price level represents an increase in the burden of debtors. The creditor is benefited, but *not at the expense* of the debtor.

In the case of an increase in the price level due to a fall in productivity the scenario is the inverse. Now the debtor faces a lower cost of the fixed debt contract, but his real income has fallen. In this case the creditor loses, *but not at the expense* of the debtor because nominal income has not changed. The reason why the creditor wins or loses in each one of these two scenarios is because of changes in real income (output), not because of wealth transfers between the creditor and the debtor.

If in either scenario both parties would have had perfect foresight and been able to foresee changes in productivity, then the associated price change would already be included in the fixed debt contract. Because the Fisher Effect and the real income offset each other, the debtor might well be willing to accept the same interest rate in each one of these scenarios; either because a higher real cost of the debt happens with a higher real income, or because a lower real cost of the debt happens with a lower real income.

It follows, then, that if the monetary authority wants to minimize the wealth transfer between debtor and creditors it should follow a nominal income target policy rather than a zero inflation policy. The monetary authority cannot undo real shocks to AS, but it can produce wealth transfers between debtors and creditors by moving the AD as reaction to a movement of AS. Consider in particular the effects that would have a fall in productivity (armed conflict, bad weather in an agricultural economy, a natural disaster, etc.) that increases the price level (a fall in the price of money) and therefore the monetary authority contracts money supply to keep the price level stable. The cost of such a target is to produce an even larger fall in the level of output (and therefore a higher unemployment rate).

Notes

1 FSDP equals domestic NGDP (without exports and imports) minus change in private inventories.
2 I borrow the denomination "Hayek's rule" from Gustavson (2001).
3 In financial terms, a reduction in discount rates increases the present value of different investment projects differently because each project's cash-flow will have a different *duration*. Financial *duration*, in turn, has the dual meaning of representing an average period of production (Macaulay duration) and a measure of the present value sensitivity to changes in the discount rate (modified duration). Both concepts are associated to Böhm–Bawerk's *roundaboutness*. See Cachanosky and Lewin (2014; 2016) and Lewin and Cachanosky (2016).
4 On the *real bills doctrine* see Selgin (1989) and Timberlake (2005).
5 Hayek (1931, p. 105, emphasis added): "If the considerations brought forward in the last lecture are at all correct, it would appear that the reasons commonly advanced as a proof that the quantity of the circulating medium should vary as production increases or decreases are *entirely unfounded*. It would appear rather that the fall of prices proportionate to the increase in productivity [...] is in fact the only means of avoiding misdirection of production."
6 See, for instance, Bean (1983), Bradley and Jansen (1989), Feldstein and Stock (1994), Garín, Lester, and Sims (2016), Hall and Mankiw (1994), Kahn (1988), and McCallum (2011).
7 The precise relationship is the following: $\dot{M} + \dot{V}_Y + \dot{M} \cdot \dot{V}_Y = \pi^* + \dot{Y}_{LT} + \pi^* \cdot \dot{Y}_{LT}$, where $\dot{M} \cdot \dot{V}_Y \approx 0$ and $\pi^* \cdot \dot{Y}_{LT} \approx 0$, and therefore $\dot{M} + \dot{V}_Y$ and $\pi^* + \dot{Y}_{LT}$ are approximately equal.
8 See also the discussion in Selgin (1997, pp. 49–53).
9 A reason to call this outcome of monetary equilibrium the "*productivity* norm" is because of its application to historical cases with productivity gains. It is not meant to imply that MV is to remain constant only with an increase in *TFP*.
10 Selgin (1997, pp. 72–73) offers a similar discussion through a slightly different approach. Also see Bean (1983).
11 For instance, in the U.S. the price of houses is not part of the CPI, and transactions of used goods or stocks are not part of the GDP deflator.

References

Atkenson, A., and Kehoe, P. J. (2004). Deflation and Depression: Is There an Empirical Link? *The American Economic Review*, 94.(2): 99–103.
Bean, C. R. (1983). Targeting Nominal Income: An Appraisal. *The Economic Journal*, 93.(372): 806–819.
Bradley, M. D., and Jansen, D. W. (1989). The Optimality of Nominal Income Targeting When Wages Are Indexed to Price. *Southern Economic Journal*, 56.(1): 13–23.
Cachanosky, N., and Lewin, P. (2014). Roundaboutness Is not a Mysterious Concept: A Financial Application to Capital Theory. *Review of Political Economy*, 26.(4): 648–665.
Cachanosky, N., and Lewin, P. (2016). Financial Foundations of Austrian Business Cycle Theory. *Advances in Austrian Economics*, 20: 15–44.

Christensen, L. (2011). Market Monetarist: The Second Monetarist Counter-revolution. Retrieved from http://thefaintofheart.files.wordpress.com/2011/09/market-monetarism-13092011.pdf

DeLong, B. (1990). "Liquidation" Cycles: Old-Fashioned Real Business Cycle Theory and The Great Depression. *NBER Working Paper Series No. 3546*. Cambridge: NBER.

DeLong, B. (1998). Fiscal Policy in the Shadow of the Great Depression. In M. D. Bordo, C. Goldin, and E. N. White (Eds), *The Defining Moment: The Great Depression and American Economy in the Twentieth Century* (pp. 67–85). Chicago: University of Chicago Press.

Evans, A. J., and Thorpe, R. (2013). The (Quantity) Theory of Money and Credit. *The Review of Austrian Economics*, 26.(4): 463–481.

Feldstein, M., and Stock, J. H. (1994). The Use of a Monetary Aggregate to Target Nominal GDP. In G. Mankiw (Ed.), *Monetary Policy* (pp. 7–69). Chicago: University of Chicago Press.

Friedman, M., and Schwartz, A. J. (1982). *Monetary Trends in the United States and the United Kingdom: Their Relation to Income, Prices, and Interest Rates, 1867–1975*. Chicago: Chicago University Press.

Garín, J., Lester, R., and Sims, E. (2016). On the Desirability of Nominal GDP Targeting. *Journal of Economic Dynamics and Control*, 69: 21–44.

Giffen, R. (1904). *Economic Inquiries and Studies*. London: George Bell and Sons.

Gustavson, M. (2001). The Hayek Rule: A New Monetary Policy Framework for the 21st Century. *Policy Study No. 389*. Los Angeles: Reason Foundation.

Hall, R. E., and Mankiw, G. (1994). Nominal Income Targeting. In G. Mankiw (Ed.), *Monetary Policy1* (pp. 71–94). Chicago: University of Chicago Press.

Hayek, F. A. (1931). *Prices and Production* (1967 ed.). New York: Augustus M. Kelley.

Hayek, F. A. (1937). *Monetary Nationalism and International Stability* (1989 ed.). Fairfield: Augustus M. Kelley.

Horwitz, S. G. (1990). A Subjectivist Approach to the Demand for Money. *Journal Des Economistes et Des Etudes Humaines*, 1.(4): 459–471.

Horwitz, S. G. (2000). *Microfoundations and Macroeconomics: An Austrian Perspective* (2003 ed.). London and New York: Routledge.

Hutt, W. H. (1956). The Yield from Money Held. In M. Sennholz (Ed.), *On Freedom and Free Enterprise: Essays in Honor of Ludwig von Mises* (pp. 196–216). Princeton: Van Nostrand.

Kahn, G. (1988). Nominal GNP: An Anchor for Monetary Policy? *Economic Review*, (November): 18–35.

Lewin, P., and Cachanosky, N. (2016). A Financial Framework for Understanding Macroeconomic Cycles. *Journal of Financial Economic Policy*, 8.(2): 268–280.

McCallum, B. T. (2011). Nominal NGDP Targeting. *Shadow Open Market Committee*.

Niskanen, W. A. (1992). Political Guidance on Monetary Policy. *Cato Journal*, 12.(1): 281–286.

Niskanen, W. A. (2001). A Test of the Demand Rule. *Cato Journal*, 21.(2): 205–209.

Rothbard, M. N. (1963). *America's Great Depression* (2000 ed.). Auburn: Ludwig von Mises Institute.

Selgin, G. A. (1989). The Analytical Framework of the Real Bills Doctrine. *Journal of Institutions and Theoretical Economics*, 145.(3): 489–507.

Selgin, G. A. (1996). *Bank Deregulation and Monetary Order* (2002 ed.). New York: Routledge.

Selgin, G. A. (1997). *Less Than Zero*. London: The Institute of Economic Affairs.

Sumner, S. (2012). The Case for Nominal GDP Targeting. *Mercatus Research*. Arlington: George Mason University.

Timberlake, R. H. (2005). Gold Standard and the Real Bills Doctrine in U.S. Monetary Policy. *Econ Journal Watch*, 2.(2): 196–233.

White, L. H. (2008). Did Hayek and Robbins Deepen the Great Depression? *Journal of Money, Credit and Banking*, 40.(4): 751–768.

3   Nominal income targeting and monetary rules

Introduction

The previous chapter discussed two versions of a nominal income targeting rule: NGDP Targeting and Hayek's rule. These types of rules, however, are not among the most popular among central banks around the world. For policy makers to reconsider what monetary rules or guiding principle they should follow then a clear advantage of a nominal income target rule over other more prevalent alternatives should be clear. A comparison of a nominal income targeting rule with other widespread rules is the topic of this chapter.

In particular, the rules discussed are inflation targeting, Friedman's k-percent, McCallum's rule, and Taylor's rule. Beside a discussion of each rule, each section also compares each one of these prescriptions with a nominal income target rule to explore to what extent nominal income targeting outperforms these other rules. A central bank that follows a rule not only needs to *execute* it properly, it also needs to choose the *right* rule. The proper execution of the wrong rule can produce economic imbalances if it is the case that the chosen rule is not properly targeting monetary equilibrium.

However, before discussing the above-mentioned rules, a few reflections on the debate on rules versus discretion in monetary policy are needed. If nominal income targeting is still a rule, then the case for rules over discretion in the realm of monetary policy can stand on firmer ground. To understand this situation, it is necessary to review a few characteristics of the rules-versus-discretion debate.

Rules versus discretion in monetary policy

If we take as given the presence of a monetary authority such as a central bank, and also that a perfect rule perfectly executed is not feasible, then said central bank needs to decide if it is going to nonetheless follow a monetary rule or if it is going to have discretion in how monetary policy should be executed on a case-by-case basis. The underlying question in this debate is which approach to monetary policy minimizes the mistakes we already know that the monetary authority is going to commit.[1] But it is also possible that a discretionary central bank can perform as well as the best monetary rule in normal times and outperform the monetary rule during a more unstable situation that is not properly taken into consideration by the design of this rule. Unexpected shocks could be an example of situations where discretion could, in principle, outperform a monetary rule.

Arguably, since the economy is a complex system subject to unexpected shocks and uncertainty, a discretionary monetary authority might be preferred to be able to deal with events that cannot be foreseen in a rule. This case for discretion, however, is not as straightforward as it seems to be. A reason for this is that, if the market is as complex as the discretionary side argues, then the chances of making things worse are being undervalued by assuming that the monetary authority can outperform the rule precisely during more complex times. Namely, the policy maker is able to successfully deal with a rare situation in a complex environment but is at the same time assumed to be unable to make things worse. It is for this complexity reason that advocates of rules prefer to follow rules *even* in non-normal situations. Another reason is that, as the 1920s Strong Hearings in the United States show, policy making can be subject to political pressure, personality issues, and typical public choice problems among other factors. A rule would also protect monetary policy from these factors. In this line of argument, a rule is needed for a central bank to remain independent from the government.

Yet another challenge can still be put in front of the discretionary position. The strongest scenario in favor of discretionary behavior is in the case of an unexpected shock that takes economic agents by surprise. This unexpected shock can either be a nominal or a real one. If it is a nominal shock, and is unexpected, then its source is some sort of irrational behavior (i.e. Keynes's animal spirits). In the case of a fall in spending, then the central bank may see the need to step out of the rule and increase money supply to offset the fall in aggregate demand (AD). It is no surprise the Keynesian leaning economists are more sympathetic to discretion while their monetarist peers are more sympathetic to the central bank being committed to a strict rule. Now, the case of an unexpected nominal shock that has its origin in a sort of irrational behavior begs three questions.

The first one, which is a general issue for these explanations, is why economic agents are irrational and where the irrationality is coming from. Note that in this case irrationality needs to be important enough to produce an economic crisis. The second one is why would irrational economic agents react rationally to the central bank's discretionary steps. And, if economic agents are irrational, then it is not clear how the central bank would be able to predict the behavior of the irrational economic agents to its rational policy. The third one is why would policy makers in charge of monetary policy be free of the same type of irrational behavior. The rationality of policy makers should not be assumed to be of a special kind. If, on the contrary, there is no such irrational behavior, then a mistaken expectation by economic agents on what the monetary authority will do cannot be the cause of a nominal shock since the behavior of AD is publicly known and follows a specific rule. The presence of a monetary rule contributes to anchor the expectations on money supply making unnecessary the discretionary powers of the monetary authority (assuming the monetary authority makes public the rule that follows). Alternatively, the possibility of a discretionary behavior by the monetary authority increases the uncertainty of the economic agents. Therefore, knowing the *reason* why there is a nominal shock is important. If agents can be irrational, then we cannot expect that these same agents will conveniently behave rationally when the central bank applies a discretionary policy or that the central banks are for some reason shielded from irrational behavior. If economic agents are always rational, then strictly following a rule minimizes the shocks since the uncertainty component of the discretionary behavior is not present.

If the shock is instead a real one, there is only so much that can be achieved with a discretionary policy even if all economic agents are rational. In the case of a negative real shock output falls and the price level increases. If the central bank can be discretionary, there are only three things it can do, (1) decrease AD, (2) increase AD, or (3) keep AD as it is (do nothing). If the central bank choses to fight the increase in the price level by decreasing AD, then the cost of this policy is to make output fall even more and make the unemployment situation even worse than doing nothing. If, on the contrary, the central bank decides to offset the fall in output by increasing AD then the cost of this policy is to increase even more the price level than doing nothing. Since this is a real shock and the long-run aggregate supply has shifted to the left, the long-run result is to have either more or less inflation, but it is not feasible to go back to the pre-shock level of output by using monetary policy. The third alternative is to let the effects of the real shock play out by themselves and not change the course of monetary policy. In the case of a real shock, then, the monetary authority cannot do away with the crisis as in the presence of a nominal shock. When facing a real shock, the monetary authority can only manage (to some extent) *how* the crisis is going to unfold.

The third option, do nothing, has an advantage over options (1) and (2). These other two alternatives impose a cost besides the extra fall in output or the extra rise in the price level by either increasing or decreasing the money supply when there is no change in money demand. The reason this is an *extra* cost is because the central bank is pushing the money market outside its equilibrium and therefore is adding a monetary disequilibrium to the real shock. Note that, as discussed in the previous chapter, in the case of a negative real shock what we have is *good inflation* just as in the case of a positive real shock what we have is a case of *good deflation*. Therefore, if the central bank does not want to add further disequilibria to an economic downturn due to a negative real shock, the monetary authority should keep AD still, and since AD equals MV (which equals NGDP), this is equivalent to holding a nominal income target rule. The superiority of a nominal income target with respect to trying to manage a real shock is that it avoids adding a monetary disequilibrium to the real negative shock. In addition, if the central bank follows a nominal income target, it does not need to go through the problem of finding out whether the fall in output is due to a nominal or real shock and risk prescribing the wrong medicine.

Inflation targeting

Under inflation targeting, a central bank commits itself to a *target*, but not to *how* the chosen target is going to be achieved. In this sense inflation targeting is not a rule because there is no technical prescription to the central bank on how to execute monetary policy, it is an explicit and public commitment that keeps the discretionary faculties of the monetary authority in place in terms of *how* to achieve the target. Inflation targeting originated after the high inflation of the late 1970s and the abandonment of the Bretton Woods arrangement. In this scenario central banks needed to find a new nominal anchor.[2] The first attempts were focused on money supply (it is in this context that Friedman proposes his k-percent rule discussed in the next section). European countries used their exchange rates as their nominal anchors (pegging their currencies to the German mark). But this arrangement ultimately failed due to a series of currency crises in the 1990s. At the same time New Zealand and Canada explicitly moved toward an inflation target regime that became an internationally popular rule for its correlation with low inflation and the lack of alternative nominal anchors. This combination of events gave the impression that discretion is a superior approach than following rules.

Bernanke, Laubach, Mishkin, and Posen (1999, Chapter 2) mention three reasons for a central bank to follow an inflation targeting policy. The first one is that policy makers agree that the control that central banks have over real variables such as unemployment and real output is more limited than some theories and models suggest, especially when moving away from the short-run toward the long-run. Alternatively, central banks also have more control on nominal variables such as the price level in the long-run. Therefore, the monetary authority would do well in aiming at the long-run stability of a variable it can in fact control.

The second one is that even when the inflation rate is not too high, there can be negative effects on the long-run trend of GDP. For instance, Perron and Wada (2005) find that there is a change in the growth rate of the U.S. GDP in 1973, just after the fall of the Bretton Woods arrangement; an event that coincides with a change in the average inflation rate of the U.S. Therefore, the inflation rate is an important variable to keep in check for the long-run performance of the economy.

The third one, and also maybe the main advantage of inflation targeting, is that if the monetary authority is trustworthy in the eyes of the economic agents, then by publicly announcing the inflation target the monetary authority aligns the inflation expectations in the market to its own policy. This contributes to minimizing how far off actual inflation expectations are and also to having the short-run aggregate supply adjust sooner to the long-run equilibrium. Furthermore, a public announcement of inflation targeting also contributes to the accountability and transparency of policy makers.

Of course, for the central bank commitment to be credible there needs to be a cost if policy makers fail to achieve the target. If there is no penalty for policy makers who fail in achieving the promised target, then the monetary authority may feel inclined to deviate from the target and cheat the public. For instance, once the monetary authority has convinced the public that inflation would be, say, 2%, the central bank can aim at a 5% inflation to achieve a short-run increase in output and a short-run fall in unemployment. For this scheme to work, policy makers themselves need to have a reputable background and be respected by public opinion and economic agents. A way to increase a central bank's creditability is not just to change its behavior from rules to discretion (or the other way around), but also to change their higher authorities when they have eroded their credibility by repeatedly cheating the public or failing to achieve the target.

This credibility issue builds into the time inconsistency problem (Barro and Gordon, 1983; Kydland and Prescott, 1977). The problem is that the central bank's incentive to hit the target disappears by announcing to the public its target. Because economic agents are as rational as the policy maker, they understand this situation just as well. It is not possible, then, for the central bank to *trick* the public by announcing a low inflation target and then producing a high inflation rate. Because the public can rationalize the monetary authority incentives, the public will automatically expect a higher inflation rate than the one announced as the target. The result is a higher inflation rate without the short-run increase in output. The role of a penalty to the policy maker, should he fail to achieve the announced target, is to change the incentives of the policy maker in a way that he would not want to deviate or *trick* the public. It is no accident that the problem of time inconsistency and the rise of rational expectations occurred in the 1970s, a decade with rising inflation rates but no output improvement.

Bernanke et al. (1999) consider inflation targeting a successful way to decrease inflation and achieve price level stability. Note that inflation targeting offers an explicit *target* but leaves the *discretionary* powers of policy makers mostly intact. Inflation targeting can be pointed out, then, as an example of how discretion can outperform rules. Beckworth (2014), however, suggests that the success of inflation targeting might be overstated and that *good luck* played an important role in its apparent success. Beckworth points out that during the 1980s and the 1990s, productivity shocks were smaller and total factor productivity was more stable, making inflation targeting an easy target to hit.[3] Furthermore, when productivity increased at a faster pace after the late 1990s we see the dot-com crisis and the 2007/08 financial crisis *absent* significant changes in price level stability. These two events show that inflation targeting, or a stable price level, does not guarantee economic stability and that central banks can in fact be misled in the presence of productivity shocks. If the apparent success of inflation targeting was not due to the good luck of having a convenient environment, then the policy makers should not have been misled by the low inflation rates during the faster pace of productivity gains.

Note that inflation targeting aims at stabilizing the price level, not nominal income. Therefore, in the presence of an increase in productivity the central bank would have to increase the money supply in order to hit the target. This expansion in money supply increases the *menu costs* in the economy overall and produces a monetary disequilibrium. In short, inflation targeting does not distinguish between *good* and *bad* deflation and does not account for changes in productivity gains.

Friedman's k-percent

Friedman's (1960; 1968) k-percent rule prescribes a constant growth rate of money supply. Friedman's rule is quite simple and its intuition is easy to capture with the quantity theory of money. Friedman's k-percent rule allows for short-run deviations of an optimal change in money supply in order to prioritize long-run equilibrium and stability. In Friedman's view, it is more important to have a publicly known and clear target, even if it is a little off the right number, than erratically adjusting money supply. Equation 3.1 shows the equation of exchange in growth rates (denoted with an upper dot).

$$\dot{M} + \dot{V} = \dot{P} + \dot{Y} \tag{3.1}$$

Since money velocity is assumed to be fairly stable, then $\dot{V} \approx 0$, then rearranging 3.1 the inflation rate is approximated by $\dot{P} \approx \dot{M} - \dot{Y}$. The point of Friedman's rule is that in every period M should grow at the long-run growth rate (or trend growth rate) of Y. The long-run growth rate of Y is the k-percent (which Friedman estimates to be between 3% and 5% for the United States). Then, on average the inflation rate equals zero as deviations of money supply with respect to money demand cancel each other. Surely, if we observe any particular time period the percentage change in M might be more or less than the percent change in Y. The error (e) of each period is $e_t = gY_t - \dot{Y}$, where gY_t is the growth rate of Y in period t. But if we look at the long-run as one single period, then $\dot{M} = \dot{Y}$ and $\sum_{t=0}^{T} e_t = 0$. The underlying argument to follow this rule is that the short-term deviations e_t that occur in any particular period are smaller than the deviation that would likely occur if the central bank had the discretionary behavior to minimize those deviation period by period. A reason for this is that the connection between changes in money supply and the price level is too loose to be precisely managed and long lags are involved. For pragmatic reasons, the monetary authority should target a k-percent growth rate for the monetary aggregate that has the more stable velocity (BM, M1, M2, etc.). A discretionary behavior would then likely add a policy-maker error component (ξ) to the error of each period t, and as long as the loss function has a quadratic form, then an increase of ξ in the error is more costly than a reduction in the loss by a similar ξ reduction of the error. Therefore, if the policy maker deviates ξ half of the time toward an increase in the error, and the other half of the time toward a reduction in the error, the overall result is an increase in the cost of all the errors. Intuitively, the policy maker needs to be better at reducing the errors than it is at making the error larger (see the appendix for a more detailed discussion).

This rule can easily be combined with an inflation target of $\dot{P}^*$. If the monetary authority considers that it is less costly to err on the side of inflation than to err on the side of deflation, then it can add an inflation target that would optimize the combination of both errors when their costs are not symmetrical. In this case, money supply should grow at k-percent plus the inflation target: $\dot{M} = \dot{Y} + \dot{P}^*$.

As long as V is actually stable, Friedman's k-percent rule looks similar to a nominal income target rule since MV will grow at a constant rate. There is, however, a conceptual difference. While Friedman's k-percent rule aims at price level stability, nominal income targeting aims at MV (or NGDP) stability and lets the price level be independent and freely move inversely to changes in productivity. Friedman's k-percent rule seems to rely on the notion that monetary equilibrium means price level stability instead of the quantity of money supplied being equal to the quantity of money demand (the constant *MV* condition). But as long as *MV* is growing, the result is a permanent monetary disequilibrium. What Friedman's k-percent rule prescribes, assuming *V* is constant, is that money supply should grow beyond money demand at the same rate as the trend of real GDP.

If Friedman's k-percent rule is extended to allow for changes in *V*, then the rule becomes $\dot{M} = \dot{Y} - \dot{V}$. If *V* were volatile but its trend constant, this would mean that the deviations of monetary policy in each particular period can be larger than just the deviation of the growth rate of *Y* with respect to the trend or long-run growth rate, but in the long-run the price level would still be stable. Now the error of the rule for each period *t* becomes $e_t = (gY_t - \dot{Y}) + (gV_t - \dot{V})$. The error in period *t* will be less than when velocity is constant in the particular case where the signs of each parenthesis are opposite to each other. This will be the case, for instance, when GDP grows more than the trend but money velocity increases less than the trend. The first component calls for an increase in money supply while the second calls for a reduction of money supply. In the particular case where GDP and velocity deviate from their trend by the same proportion, then the error for that particular period becomes zero. It is possible, at least in theory, that by mistakenly assuming a constant velocity the rule deviations are smaller than the cyclical component of *Y* as long as velocity has a constant (horizontal) trend ($\dot{V} = 0$) and its cyclical component matches the cyclical component of GDP. But Figure 3.1 shows that the assumption that *V*'s trend is constant may not hold.

If the monetary authority assumes that the trend of money velocity is constant, then Friedman's k-percent rule can go off-track in periods such as the ones seen

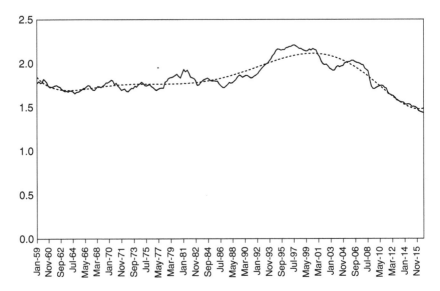

Figure 3.1 M2 velocity, United States, 1959–2015.

Source: Federal Reserve Bank of St. Louis FRED®.

since 1986 when the trend of money velocity first rises and then falls. Had the Federal Reserve calibrated Friedman's k-percent before the 1980s and it applied afterwards, it would have resulted in higher inflation than desired between the mid-1980s and the early-2000s and less inflation than desired afterwards. Assuming a constant velocity when in fact there is a trend biases the performance of Friedman's k-percent rule. But to account for changes in money velocity makes this rule harder to implement and to understand by the public.

It should still be noted, however, that the fact that Friedman's k-percent rule aims at long-run equilibrium does not mean that the short-run deviations do not matter. If either the cycle component of Y or the volatility of V are large enough, then the accumulated distortions in each period might be too large to achieve long-run equilibrium free of economic issues. Note that this case does not represent a one-time deviation in money supply with respect to money demand, but a case of a continuous sequence of deviations. Money neutrality does not imply that there are no real effects in the short-run, it rather assumes that there are no real effects in the long-run. Therefore, with errors large enough, if the accumulation of short-run real effects is significant enough the rule fails to achieve its objective. Admittedly, as seen in Figure 3.1, the likelihood of this scenario was small when Friedman was developing the k-percent rule, but such scenario changes in the early 1980s when M2 velocity starts to increase. A reason why Friedman's k-percent rule presents these issues is the absence of a clear feedback mechanism rule. Still, it should be noted again that Friedman's k-percent is an indirect way of targeting price level stability, not monetary equilibrium.

McCallum's feedback rule

McCallum (1982; 1984; 1989, pp. 336–350) shows some dissatisfaction with Friedman's k-percent rule and offers an alternative prescription. There are three reasons why McCallum is concerned with Friedman's rule. The first one is that the monetary authority should aim at variables upon which it has a large degree of control, rather than a loose control. For instance, the central bank has more control over the size of the base money than over an aggregate monetary variable such as M2. The second one is that policy makers do not have enough information to distinguish, in the short-run, how much of a change in a nominal variable such as NGDP is due to real changes and how much is due to changes in the price level. In other words, the monetary authorities cannot accurately and timely separate real from nominal effects. The third one is that Friedman's k-percent rule relies on the assumption, or hope, that once the k-percent value is decided, it will be the appropriate value indefinitely. McCallum's worry about this last point is not off-base (Figure 3.1). While Friedman argues that money velocity has been falling at an average rate of 1%, McCallum argues that M1 velocity has actually been increasing at an average rate of 2.5% between 1954 and 1986. It might be argued that Friedman's rule can be modified in a way such that the k-percent is calculated again every year (or quarter) with new information on trend of GDP and money velocity. But this would not solve the issue. The longer the time period used to estimate every year's k-percent, the slower the k-percent value will be adjusted to its optimal value. And the shorter the time horizon used to estimate the k-percent, the less accurate the separation between cycle and trend from the GDP series will be and therefore part of the cyclical behavior will be informing what the growth rate of the chosen monetary aggregate should be. The more flexible we make the k-percent, the less efficient the rule becomes. Likewise, the more efficient we make the rule, the more inflexible it becomes.

McCallum's rule includes a feedback term that would inform what the change in the growth rate of money supply would be, taking into account the three concerns mentioned above. McCallum's feedback rule is described by Equation 3.2 (where $\lambda \in (0;1)$).

$$\dot{B}_t = \dot{B}_{t-1} + \lambda(\ln(NGDP^*) - \ln(NGDP_t)) \tag{3.2}$$

McCallum's first concern is addressed by having the monetary authority target the change in monetary base (B) rather than a broader money aggregate such as M1 or M2. His second concern is addressed by having the rule focus on the behavior of NGDP rather than on the behavior of (real) GDP as Friedman's k-percent rule does. McCallum's third concern is addressed by adding a target for NGDP growth (denoted as $NGDP^*$) and by adding the parameter $\lambda \in (0,1)$. McCallum suspects that 1% would be a good growth target for NGDP.

Consider first the case where NGDP is at the desired level, in that case the growth rate of monetary base in the present period equals the growth rate of the monetary base in the last period. As long as NGDP equals the desired target value then McCallum's rule prescribes a constant growth rate of money base as Friedman's k-percent rule would do if applied to the monetary base as well. However, as long as nominal income is out of target the growth rate of base money in the present period will be corrected upward (downward) if NGDP is above (below) target. The role of λ is to calibrate how much the growth rate of base money should change when NGDP deviates from its target (MacCallum suggests $\lambda = 0.25$). Because of this, McCallum cautions that to have a rule does not imply inaction by the monetary authority. Advocates of a discretionary central bank should not object to rules if they do not allow for any adjustment of money supply (the case of Friedman's k-percent).

By focusing on NGDP instead of GDP, and by setting a target, McCallum's feedback rule can also be a type of nominal income target. A way to more clearly see the resemblance is to open the money aggregate M from Equation 3.3 into base money times the money multiplier (m) as seen on the left-hand side in Equation 3.3.

$$BmV_t = NGDP_t + \lambda(NGDP_{t-1} - NGDP^*_{t-1}) \tag{3.3}$$

McCallum's feedback rule focuses on the behavior of B while nominal income targeting focuses on the behavior of MV (or BmV). MacCallum's rule, however, revolves around targeting NGDP. This means that how much B should change to hit the NGDP target is not independent of what is happening to mV. This is why a nominal income targeting rule can be interpreted as a generalization of McCallum's feedback rule where m and V are allowed to change. Alternatively, McCallum's feedback rule can be interpreted as a suggestion to use B as the variable of choice to keep MV stable and return it to its level after a deviation occurs.

Taylor's rule

Instead of looking at a monetary aggregate, Taylor's (1993) rule focus is on the interest rate used as a target by a central bank, usually a short-term rate like the federal funds rate in the United States. A reason for this is that Taylor is actually evaluating the Federal Reserve's monetary policy and therefore uses as its target or dependent variable the same target used by the Federal Reserve. Arguably, Taylor's rule is more an *ex post* evaluation of monetary policy than an *ex ante* prescription. In other words, Taylor develops a "hypothetical but representative" rule that "approximates the Federal Reserve policy during the past recent years" (p. 195). Since then, a large body of literature has developed that recommends applying Taylor's rule as a mandate of monetary policy and its effectiveness.[4] Many modifications to the original Taylor rule have been proposed, Taylor's own representation in 1993 is also referred as the *classic* Taylor rule and is represented in Equation 3.4:

$$i_t = r_t + \pi_t + \alpha_\pi (\pi_t - \pi^*) + \alpha_y (y_t - \bar{y}) \tag{3.4}$$

where i is the short-term interest rate targeted by the monetary authority, r is the real interest rate of equilibrium, π is the GDP deflation inflation over the last four quarters, π^* is the inflation target, y is the log of real GDP, $\bar{y}$ is the log of potential output, and the α are positive coefficients. Taylor's (1993) rule with his own parameters becomes $i_t = 2\% + \pi_t + 0.5(\pi_t - 2\%) + 0.5(y_t - \bar{y})$.

Taylor's rule can be interpreted as adding two correction terms to Fisher's equation: $i = r + \pi$. These two correction terms are the inflation gap and the output gap. While Fisher's equation uses the *expected* inflation and Taylor's rule uses the *past* inflation, this difference can be saved in the scenario where each quarter inflation is around the target and therefore the expected inflation is similar to the historical or past inflation. Consider the case where inflation equals the desired target and there is no output gap, in that case Taylor's rule's prescription for the interest rate becomes $i_t = r_t + \pi_t$. But if inflation is below (above) target and output is below (above) its potential, then the federal funds rate should decrease (increase) by both gaps by the α weight associated to each deviation. In Taylor's own representation, both weights are equal to 0.5. But it could be the case that a monetary authority decides to react more to an output gap than to an inflation gap (or the other way around). This way, Taylor's rule prescribes lowering the interest rate, as a discretionary central bank would likely prescribe in a similar situation, but it specifies a precise amount that comes from a rule. In this sense, Taylor's rule is providing a constraint to the same behavior a discretionary policy maker would have.

Taylor (2007; 2009a; 2009b; 2010) argues that an important reason for the 2007–8 financial crisis in the U.S. was a significant deviation from the classic Taylor rule which ignited the housing bubble. Ahrend, Cournède, and Price (2008) find that those countries that deviated most from their Taylor rules had larger housing bubbles as well. Also, Cachanosky (2015) notes that the two largest economic downturns in Latin America coincide with the two largest U.S. deviations from Taylor's rule.[5] Empirical studies show a correlation between deviations from the Taylor rule and economic imbalances.

Despite its popularity and empirical support, it is not easy for a central bank to adopt Taylor's rule. The first limitation is no less than knowing the value of the natural or equilibrium real interest rate. The natural interest rate is not observable, and this is precisely what the rule is targeting. The point of the rule is to set the nominal interest rate such that it is aligned with the assumed real interest rate of equilibrium (save for adjustments in the case of inflation or output gap). Therefore, Taylor's rule would prescribe a biased nominal interest rate if the assumed real interest rate is significantly incorrect. While in principle the real interest rate can be approximated with the long-run growth of real output or by subtracting inflation from nominal interest rates, these values are not independent of changes in money supply prescribed by the Taylor rule.

The second limitation is not having real-time access to inflation and output gap information as the rule requires. One way to deal with this issue is to replace these variables with other ones that are more readily available like CPI or core-CPI for inflation and unemployment and the natural rate of unemployment for the output gap. Of course, this still means that the monetary authority should have a reliable estimation of the natural rate of unemployment as well. Other solutions, like an index of a composite of inflation and output measures could be used as well instead of relying on a single proxy if it is not clear which of all the potential indices is the most efficient one.

The above-mentioned limitations point to the issue of having good real-time information for the rule to be operational and not an *ex post* way to analyze how a central bank performed in the past. There is, however, a third limitation, which is the way this rule handles productivity shocks. In the case of productivity gains, the output gap increases not because output falls, but because potential output increases. Similarly, inflation falls behind the desired target, not because there is a shortage of money supply, but because productivity gains make the price of final goods fall (*good* deflation). In this scenario of productivity gains, Taylor's rule prescribes an increase in money supply, and therefore produces a monetary disequilibrium when this is not needed. In a simple textbook-type of analysis it is assumed that output increases automatically with an increase in productivity and that therefore there is no gap to fill. In the real-world of policy making, this may not be the case. The result is that monetary policy gets in the way of resource allocation during a time of changes in productivity. Even if the output gap is closed automatically, the inflation gap term would prescribe a reduction in the short-term interest rate. In this case the rule should update the inflation target to account for the productivity shock as a way to close the gap, instead of raising the observed inflation to match an inflation target that implicitly assumes no productivity shocks. In this scenario, a reduction of the interest rate would produce the same effect that the Taylor rule is trying to avoid in the first place.

Consider two differences with a nominal income target rule. The first one is that in the case of productivity shock (positive or negative), nominal income targeting does not prescribe a change in monetary policy because there is no monetary disequilibrium to fix. The second one is that this type of rule *does not require* the monetary authority to know the value of the natural or real interest rate of equilibrium. A nominal income target rule is more efficient than a Taylor rule in the sense that it is less dependent on variables that are non-observable, and it distinguishes between nominal and real shocks. It should be said, however, that the Taylor rule's original intent was to *map* the past behavior of the Federal Reserve more than to design a rule to be followed by central banks.

Challenges of applying rules

Why are rules not applied?

Given the reasons discussed above, McCallum (1989) points to two reasons why rules lack popularity among central banks. The first one, though not very likely, is to confuse a rule with a passive behavior, namely a rule without a feedback mechanism such as Friedman's k-percent. A rule as rigid as Friedman's can indefinitely set monetary policy off-track. Better would be to rely on the policy makers' discretion.

The second reason relates to how the policy makers see themselves. The image of the head of a central bank as the second most powerful person of a country vanishes if all they must do is follow a rule that a modern computer can perform just as well as them. The central banker, then, should bring some value added on top of a rule, and that is their discretionary judgment. These incentives can lead to a self-selection process of pro-discretion monetary economists to work at central banks. With some resemblance to capture theory, White (2005) argues that the Federal Reserve funding into monetary economics is likely to have an influence on the research orientation of this field.

Easy rules versus complex rules

White (1999, pp. 225–226) also points to another important difficulty of applying rules, which is a trade-off between easy and complex rules and accountability of the policy maker. The simpler the rule is, the more accountable the policy maker can be held. But the simpler the rule, the more likely it will be an inefficient prescription. As we've seen, Friedman's k-percent can be set off-track when money velocity changes. An even more rigid rule would be to freeze the monetary base. With this rule it is very easy to hold the policy maker accountable for changes in the base money.

A more complex rule, such as McCallum's feedback rule, Taylor's rule, or a nominal income target rule, makes it more elusive to hold policy makers accountable. Let us say, for instance, that the central bank follows an NGDP Targeting rule. When facing a change in velocity, the policy maker must decide *how* to adjust money supply and by how *much*. For instance, this can be done by changing reserve requirements or the monetary base. If the policy maker misses the target, they can argue that it was due to unforeseeable external effects that affected money velocity, and not his wrongdoing. In other words, the more complex the rule is, the more loopholes that can be used to excuse the policy maker for missing the target. However, the challenges of holding policy makers accountable for their results should not be allowed to get in the way of applying an appropriate rule and macroeconomic stability.

Appendix

Friedman's k-percent rule loss function

Assume a simple quadratic loss function where the loss value (L) equals the squared value of the errors of the policy. An error is a deviation of a change in money supply due to a difference between the actual change of GDP and money velocity with their respective trends. The quadratic form of the loss function produces two effects. First, a loss occurs either if there is a shortage or a surplus of money supply with respect to the ideal for each period t. Second, larger deviations produce increasing values of loss. For simplicity, also assume that the loss function is symmetric, meaning that the loss of 2% inflation equals the loss of a 2% deflation. Equations 3.5 and 3.6 represent the error and loss function.

$$e = (gY - \dot{Y}) + (gV - \dot{V}) + \xi = (e_Y + e_V + \xi) \tag{3.5}$$

$$L = e^2 = (e_Y + e_V + \xi)^2 \tag{3.6}$$

where gY and $\dot{Y}$ represent the actual growth of GDP and the long-run growth of GDP respectively.

The same interpretation applies to money velocity (V). The error of the discretionary policy maker is denoted by ξ. For simplicity, these equations also assume that errors with respect to growth rate of Y and percent changes in V are equally weighted. Consider first the case where the monetary authority does not have discretionary powers and strictly follows Friedman's k-percent rule. In this case $\xi = 0$ (discretion neither increases nor decreases the loss of the rule). Then, the loss in any period t is represented by Equation 3.7.

$$L = e_Y^2 + e_V^2 + 2 \cdot e_Y e_V \tag{3.7}$$

Note that if the signs of $e_{Y,t}$ and $e_{V,t}$ are opposite to each other, then the value of the loss is reduced through the third term. If money velocity is constant, then

$L = e_Y^2$. But if money velocity is not constant, then it is possible that the total loss is reduced if $|2 \cdot e_Y e_V| > e_V^2$.

Consider now the case where the monetary authority has the discretionary power of trying to improve upon Friedman's k-percent rule. The monetary authority can either increase or decrease the error in each period t depending on the sign of ξ. According to Equation 3.5, the loss becomes zero when $\xi = -(e_Y + e_V)$. Equation 3.8 shows the loss value when $\xi \neq 0$.

$$L = e_Y^2 + e_V^2 + \xi^2 + 2 \cdot e_Y e_V + 2 \cdot e_Y \xi + 2 \cdot e_V \xi \tag{3.8}$$

If the policy maker is skilled enough, then it can improve upon a strict obedience of Friedman's k-percent rule when $e_Y^2 + e_V^2 + 2 \cdot e_Y e_V \geq e_Y^2 + e_V^2 + \xi^2 + 2 \cdot e_Y e_V + 2 \cdot e_Y \xi + 2 \cdot e_V \xi$. This means that discretionary behavior improves upon Friedman's k-percent rule if $0 \geq \xi(\xi + 2e_Y + 2e_V)$. This occurs when $\xi \leq -2(e_Y + e_V)$. This means that the policy maker can improve upon Friedman's k-percent rule if its discretionary involvement offsets by no more than two times the combined error terms. Otherwise, the total error would fall on the other side and farther away from the optimal behavior of money supply.

To end with, consider the impact on the total loss when the central bank has discretionary powers and in the first period increases the error of the policy ($\xi > 0$) and in the second period it reduces the error of the policy by the same amount ($\xi < 0$) (in addition the size of the discretionary error is less than two times the deviation of the rule). Equations 3.9 and 3.10 show the change in the total loss of these two situations respectively.

$$\Delta^+ L = \xi^2 + 2 \cdot e_Y \xi + 2 \cdot e_V \xi > 0 \tag{3.9}$$

$$\Delta^- L = \xi^2 - 2 \cdot e_Y \xi - 2 \cdot e_V \xi < 0 \tag{3.10}$$

For clarity, the negative sign of ξ in Equation 3.10 is captured as the negative signs in front of the second and third terms. Equations 3.9 and 3.10 show that the same size of discretionary error increases losses more than it reduces them. This means that $\Delta^+ L + \Delta^- L = 2\xi^2 > 0$. The conditions required for a discretionary policy maker to outperform a simple rule as Friedman's k-percent should not be taken for granted even in a simple scenario as the one presented here.

Notes

1 The debate on rules versus discretion in monetary policy is hardly new. The issue was discussed in the U.S. in the 1920s Strong Hearings held by the House Committee on Banking and Currency. Simons (1936) is probably the first academic discussion. For more reviews on this debate see Brunner and Meltzer (1993), Buchanan (1983), Christ (1983), Dwyer (1993), Fisher (1988), Hetzel (1985), Kocherlakota (2016), and Ravier (2008).

2 Since fiat money has no value of use, and virtually a zero-marginal cost of producing an extra dollar, central banks need a nominal anchor that would constrain the supply of money and define the price level.

3 Beckworth (2014) builds on Cecchetti and Ehrmann (2002), Mishkin and Schmidt-Hebbel (2007), and Walsh (2009). Their research shows that the *good luck* hypothesis can explain the apparent success of inflation targeting and the stability of the Great Moderation era.

4 For a sample see Ahrend, Cournède, and Price (2008), Kozicki (1999), Leith and Wren-Lewis (2009), Martins (2000), Molodtsova, Nikolsko-Rzhevskyy, and Papell (2011), Orphanides (2007), and Woodford (2001).

5 For a sample of research related to Latin American business cycle see Aiolfi, Catão, and Timmermann (2011), Cachanosky (2014), Calvo, Leiderman, and Reinhart (1993; 1994), Calvo and Talvi (2008), Canova (2005), Gallego, Gardó, Martin, Molina, and Serena (2010), Izquierdo and Talvi (2008), Jara, Moreno, and Tovar (2009), and Ocampo (2009, 2010).

References

Ahrend, R., Cournède, B., and Price, R. (2008). Monetary Policy, Market Excesses and Financial Turmoil. *Economics Department Working Paper No. 597*. OECD.

Aiolfi, M., Catão, L. A. V., and Timmermann, A. (2011). Common Factors in Latin America's Business Cycles. *Journal of Development Economics*, 95.(2): 212–228.

Barro, R. J., and Gordon, D. B. (1983). A Positive Theory of Monetary Policy in a Natural Rate Model. *Journal of Political Economy*, 91.(4): 589–610.

Beckworth, D. (2014). Inflation Targeting: A Monetary Policy Regime Whose Time Has Come and Gone. *Mercatus Research*. Arlington: George Mason University.

Bernanke, B. S., Laubach, T., Mishkin, F. S., and Posen, A. S. (1999). *Inflation Targeting: Lessons from the International Experience*. Princeton and Oxford: Princeton University Press.

Brunner, K., and Meltzer, A. H. (1993). *Money and the Economy: Issues in Monetary Analysis*. Cambridge: Cambridge University Press.

Buchanan, J. M. (1983). Monetary Research, Monetary Rules, and Monetary Regimes. *Cato Journal*, 3.(1): 143–146.

Cachanosky, N. (2014). The Effects of U.S. Monetary Policy on Colombia and Panama (2002–2007). *The Quarterly Review of Economics and Finance*, 54: 428–436.

Cachanosky, N. (2015). U.S. Monetary Policy's Impact on Latin America's Structure of Production (1960–2010). *Latin American Journal of Economics*, 51.(2): 95–116.

Calvo, G. A., Leiderman, L., and Reinhart, C. M. (1993). Capital Inflows and Real Exchange Rate Appreciation in Latin America: The Role of External Factors. *Staff Papers*, 40.(1): 108–151.

Calvo, G. A., Leiderman, L., and Reinhart, C. M. (1994). Capital Inflows to Latin America: The 1970s and the 1990s. In E. L. Bacha (Ed.), *Economics in a Changing World* (pp. 123–148). London: Macmillan.

Calvo, G. A., and Talvi, E. (2008). Sudden Stop, Financial Factors and Economic Collpase in Latin America: Learning from Argentina and Chile. In N. Serra and J. E. Stiglitz (Eds), *The Washington Consensus Reconsidered: Towards a New Global Governance* (pp. 119–149). New York: Oxford University Press.

Canova, F. (2005). The Transmission of US Shocks to Latin America. *Journal of Applied Econometrics*, 20.(2). 229–251.

Cecchetti, S. G., and Ehrmann, M. (2002). Does Inflation Targeting Increase Output Volatility?: An International Comparison of Policymakers' Preferences and Outcomes. In N. Loayza and K. Schmidt-Hebbel (Eds), *Monetary Policy: Rules and Transmission Mechanisms* (pp. 247–274). Series on Central Banking, Analysis, and Economic Policies, Santiago. 2002.

Christ, C. (1983). Rules Vs. Discretion in Monetary Policy. *Cato Journal*, 3.(1): 121–141.

Dwyer, G. P. J. (1993). Rules and Discretion in Monetary Policy. *Federal Reserve Bank of St. Louis Review*, 75.(3): 3–13.

Fisher, S. (1988). Rules Versus Discretion in Monetary Policy. *NBER Working Paper Series No. 2515*. Cambridge: NBER.

Friedman, M. (1960). *A Program for Monetary Stability*. New York: Fordham University Press.

Friedman, M. (1968). The Role of Monetary Policy. *The American Economic Review*, 58.(1): 1–17.

Gallego, S., Gardó, S., Martin, R., Molina, L., and Serena, J. M. (2010). The Impact of the Global Economic and Financial Crisis on Central Eastern and South Eastern Europe (CESEE) and Latin America. *Documentos Ocasionales, 1002*. Madrid: Banco de España.

Hetzel, R. L. (1985). The Rules Versus Discretion Debate Over Monetary Policy in the 1920s. *Federal Reserve Bank of Richmond Economic Review*, (November/December): 3–14.

Izquierdo, A., and Talvi, E. (2008). All That Glitters May Not Be Gold: Assessing Latin America's Recent Macroeconomic Performance. *Inter-American Development Bank*.

Jara, A., Moreno, R., and Tovar, C. E. (2009). The Global Crisis and Latin America: Financial Impact and Policy Responses. *BIS Quarterly Review*, (June): 53–68.

Kocherlakota, N. R. (2016). Rules versus Discretion: A Reconsideration. *Brookings Papers on Economic Activity*, BPEA Conference Draft, September 15–16, 2016.

Kozicki, S. (1999). How Useful Are Taylor Rules? *Economic Review*, 84.(2): 5–33.

Kydland, F. E., and Prescott, E. C. (1977). Rules Rather than Discretion: The Inconsistency of Optimal Plans. *Journal of Political Economy*, 85.(3): 473–492.

Leith, C., and Wren-Lewis, S. (2009). Taylor Rules in the Open Economy. *European Economic Review*, 53.(8): 971–995.

Martins, F. (2000). Taylor Rules. *Economic Bulletin*, (March): 49–57.

McCallum, B. T. (1982). Macroeconomics After a Decade of Rational Expectations: Some Critical Issues. *Economic Review*, November/D: 3–12.

McCallum, B. T. (1984). Monetarist Rules in the Light of Recent Experience. *American Economic Review*, 74.(2): 388–391.

McCallum, B. T. (1989). *Monetary Economuics: Theory and Policy*. New York: Macmillan Publishing Company.

Mishkin, F. S., and Schmidt-Hebbel, K. (2007). Does Inflation Targeting Make a Difference? In F. S. Mishkin, K. Schmidht-Hebbel, and N. Loayza (Eds), *Monetary Policy under Inflation Targeting* (pp. 291–372). Santiago de Chile: Banco Central de Chile.

Molodtsova, T., Nikolsko-Rzhevskyy, A., and Papell, D. H. (2011). Taylor Rules and the Euro. *Journal of Money, Credit and Banking*, 43.(2–3): 535–552.

Ocampo, J. A. (2009). Latin America and the Global Financial Crisis. *Cambridge Journal of Economics*, 33.(4): 703–724.

Ocampo, J. A. (2010). *How Well has Latin America Fared During the Global Financial Crisis?* James A Baker III Institute for Public Policy. Houston, TX: Rice University.

Orphanides, A. (2007). *Taylor Rules* (Finance and Economics Discussion Series No. 18). Washington, DC: Federal Reserve Board.

Perron, P., and Wada, T. (2005). Trend and Cycles: A New Approach and Explanations of Some Old Puzzles. *Computing in Economics and Finance, No. 252*. Society for Computational Economics.

Ravier, A. O. (2008). Regla Monetaria vs. Discrecionalidad: Una Ampliación del Debate. *Revista de Instituciones, Ideas Y Mercados*, 48: 113–148.

Simons, H. C. (1936). Rules vesus Authorities in Monetary Policy. *The Journal of Political Economy*, 44.(1): 1–30.

Taylor, J. B. (1993). Discretion versus Policy Rules in Practice. *Carnegie-Rochester Conference Series on Public Policy*, 39: 195–214.

Taylor, J. B. (2007). Housing and Monetary Policy. *Federal Reserve of Kansas City Proceedings*, 463–476.

Taylor, J. B. (2009a). Economic Policy and the Financial Crisis: An Empirical Analysis of What Went Wrong. *Critical Review*, 21.(2–3): 341–364. http://doi.org/10.1080/08913810902974865

Taylor, J. B. (2009b). *Getting Off Track*. Stanford: Hoover Institute Press.

Taylor, J. B. (2010). Getting Back on Track: Macroeconomic Policy Lessons from the Financial Crisis. *Federal Reserve Bank of St. Louis Review*, 92.(3): 165–176.

Walsh, C. E. (2009). Inflation Targeting: What Have We Learned? *International Finance*, 12.(2): 195–233.

White, L. H. (1999). *The Theory of Monetary Institutions*. Oxford: Basil Blackwell.

White, L. H. (2005). The Federal Reserve System's Influence on Research in Monetary Economics. *Econ Journal Watch*, 2.(2): 325–354.

Woodford, B. M. (2001). The Taylor Rule and Optimal Monetary Policy. *American Economic Review Papers and Proceedings*, 91.(2): 232–238.

4   Nominal income targeting and monetary disequilibrium

Introduction

The previous chapters discuss the conditions of monetary equilibrium and how nominal income targeting rules compare to other more widespread monetary rules. It was also argued that alternative rules to nominal income targeting achieve monetary equilibrium under special, albeit in some cases unrealistic, conditions. But it is also possible that a nominal income rule is executed with the wrong target and, therefore, it will also produce monetary disequilibrium. This chapter discusses the effects or symptoms of monetary disequilibrium in this scenario. In other words, what occurs when a nominal income has a target that is too high or too loose a monetary policy. The chapter also discusses the possibility that it is possible that the 5% growth rate of the United States' NGDP in the years prior to the 2008 crisis was the result of loose monetary policy. In other words, should the Federal Reserve had followed a 5% NGDP Targeting rule after the year 2001, it is likely that target would not achieve monetary equilibrium.

The usual diagnosis of monetary policy evaluates the behavior of consumer prices and unemployment. The former usually consists of observing inflation (defined as a sustained increase in the price level). The latter is an estimation of the natural rate of unemployment. But the good behavior of these indicators does not imply that there is no monetary disequilibrium or economic imbalances are being built up. Recall that the 2008 crisis occurred without signs of inflation or high unemployment.

This chapter first discusses NGDP deviations from trend as an indication of monetary policy being too loose. Second it studies the difference between Gross Domestic Product (GDP) and Gross Output (GO) as competitive measures in the estimation of monetary equilibrium. Third the discussion moves to the effects of monetary disequilibrium in final prices with respect to intermediate prices. The fourth section deals with the case where an excess of money supply is not captured by conventional price indices, potentially misleading policy makers. Finally, the fifth section looks at the problem of deviation of the interest rate from its equilibrium level.

Deviations from trend

One way to perceive if the monetary authority is being too loose on its monetary policy is to observe deviations of trend from a nominal variable such as NGDP.

When NGDP deviates from trend it is possible that the economic agents' expectations about the evolution of nominal income will not match reality and therefore their expectations will either fall short or be too optimistic. Economic agents update their demand of liquidity in terms of real cash-holding each period according to the expected inflation. Therefore, if money supply increases more than its expectation the excess will be allocated to consumption. In the real world, the situation is more complicated than just matching expectations. The fact that economic agents know that the central bank would produce inflation does not mean the costs of inflation disappear. Of course, if economic agents are expecting a situation of disequilibrium they will be better prepared to deal with the situation than if the situation is unexpected. If an individual walking in the street trips and knows he is going to fall, he can ameliorate the impact of the fall. But if he is unexpectedly pushed and falls, the impact will be harder on him. Knowing the problems ahead can better prepare us, but it does not make the problems disappear. If all that mattered was to have aligned expectations, then it would be the same to have an inflation rate of 0% or 100% as long as expectations are well aligned.

Consider the case of NGDP Targeting where it is recommended that monetary policy maintains a 5% growth of NGDP and returns to its level if there is a significant deviation. If NGDP is growing 5% a year, then *MV* is growing 5% a year. Therefore, *if* population is constant, then money supply is continuously growing at 5% more than the fall in velocity. This is a monetary disequilibrium because money supply is growing faster than money demand (the fall in money velocity). If a 5% growth rate of NGDP is the right target, then a 7% growth of NGDP would imply that the *looseness* of the monetary policy would be 2%, rather than 7% as Hayek's rule would imply (next chapter discusses the costs of Cantillon Effects).

Expectations on money supply have two components. The *level* at which NGDP should be in any given period and the *growth rate* of NGDP at any given period. This is why under an NGDP Targeting rule monetary policy should correct for both of these two deviations. This correction should be done as promptly as possible before expectations change and the monetary authority targets what now would be the wrong level of NGDP. Figure 4.1 shows the evolution of NGDP, its Hodrick–Prescott (HP) filtered trend, its deviation from trend, and its hypothetical path should it continue growing at 5% since 2008 Q3.

Note first there is an upward trend deviation before both the dotcom crisis and the 2008 financial crisis. Second, note that after the 2008 crisis NGDP falls and does not return to its original path. In fact, the change in the NGDP series is strong enough to quickly change the HP trend estimation. This figure supports the argument that a reason why the 2008 crisis was so severe is because the Federal Reserve failed to have NGDP return to its pre-crisis level soon enough and therefore nominal income fell consistently behind market expectations. Economic agents found themselves with a shortage of liquidity, cutting down consumption and investment, worsening the crisis even more. Note also that this deviation is less severe in the years prior to the dotcom crisis. The 2008 crisis will be discussed in more detail in a later chapter, for the moment it is enough to point out that this graph also delivers a challenge to the NGDP Targeting argument that the *main*

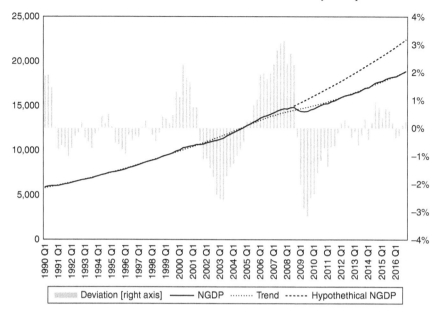

Figure 4.1 NGDP, NGDP trend, NGDP trend deviation, and hypothetical NGDP (United States).

Source: Bureau of Economic Analysis and calculations by the author. Hypothetical NGDP: NGDP grows at 5% per year starting in 2008 Q3.

reason for the 2008 crisis was NGDP falling from its level. NGDP fell in its level but remained *low* for a considerable period of time even if it kept having a stable growth rate of 4.6% between 2009 and 2015. If that is the case, then we should expect economic agents to eventually update their expectations and the crisis to be overcome as consumption increases. This reading, that the fall of NGDP is the *main* reason for the 2008 crisis, rests on expectations that might be too slow to update. It is not that economic agents do not have rational expectations, but that their adaptive expectations adjust implausibly slowly as well. This suggests that even if the NGDP Targeting argument is right about the *origin* of the crisis, it is *incomplete* with respect to the aftermath of the crisis. The severity of the Great Recession cannot be explained *only* with a nominal shock. It follows that other significant reasons besides the fall in NGDP stopped the economy from having a faster recovery.[1]

While this analysis can provide some orientation about the stance of monetary policy, it is not free of some issues as well. This analysis assumes that the HP estimation of the NGDP trend is a good proxy of NGDP equilibrium. This proxy interpretation of the HP trend may be more plausible for real series such as real GDP, but since NGDP has a nominal component and because the HP trend is calculated from NGDP in the first place, estimated trend deviation may be understated in size and display inaccurate starting points for the trend deviations. An expansionary or contractionary monetary policy can locate the NGDP series in a new path long enough for the HP trend to be affected earlier than it actually happened. This can be seen with the change of trend that starts in 2005 due to the NGDP fall of 2008. Before the fall in 2008, however, no trend deviation would have been observed even if monetary policy was indeed too loose. If the 5% growth of NGDP was too much, then the HP trend would be affected upward making the beginning point of the trend deviation appear later than it should. And because of this, the deviation will also seem to be less than it actually was. This is why the 3% trend deviation prior to the 2008 crisis might be an understatement of how loose monetary policy actually was. The following sections discuss other ways to diagnose whether monetary policy is being too loose. These other approaches can be more robust than just observing NGDP trend deviations.

Gross domestic product versus gross output

As discussed in previous chapters, in the framework of the quantity theory of money ($MV_Y = P_Y Y$) the situation of monetary equilibrium is that in which MV_Y remains constant (in per capita terms). This, however, is an approximation since in this equation money velocity, which would be the inverse of money demand, is related to the transactions of *final* goods and services only. But monetary equilibrium depends on *all* transactions rather than only on the purchases of final goods and services. And this can represent a significant challenge to the policy maker. A more proper or accurate representation would be $MV_T = P_T T$ where T denotes all the transactions that take place in an economy. This means that if the ratio Y/T is not constant, then a nominal income targeting rule based on $P_Y Y$ (NGDP) instead of $P_T T$ could be biased.

It might well be the case that during normal times the Y/T ratio is fairly stable, but this might not be the case especially during business cycles, a particular situation when central banks need to aim at the right MV to maintain aggregate demand stability. How much of a bias does it imply to target MV_Y instead of MV_T is an empirical question for which there may be no data to elucidate since macroeconomic models and variables are primarily concerned with GDP rather than total transactions. However, it should be remembered that targeting MV_Y is an empirical proxy for the actual theoretical equilibrium conditions and that this difference can leave loopholes through which signs of a monetary excess leak, misleading the policy maker about the stance of its policy.

It is this idea, that *all* transactions are important for economic stability, that lies behind (Hayek, 1931) triangular depiction of the production process. Garrison (2001, Chapter 3) offers a modern treatment of Hayek's triangle where he assumes five stages of production: (1) mining, (2) refining, (3) manufacturing, (4) distributing, and (5) retailing (Figure 4.2). Vertically, each stage of production adds value with respect to the previous stage as the production process moves forward. The total value added at the last stage of production represents what would be GDP. Because the value added of the previous stages of production is already included in the price of final goods and services, these intermediate stages of production are ignored to avoid double-counting. The downside, however, is to overlook what is happening with all the transactions in the economy.

As shown in figure 4.2, horizontally, Hayek's triangle captures time-value (where six dollars invested for one period equals two dollars invested for three periods). The hypotenuse tracks the rate at which value is added through the production process (the slope of the hypotenuse represents the interest rate). The hypotenuse, then, can also be thought as the cost of opportunity or the minimum value added (i.e. the discount rate of a cash-flow) that each stage of production should add to be profitable (note that because the hypotenuse is a straight line it is assumed that there is simple interest rate or no compounding effect).

A macroeconomic variable that also looks at intermediate investment (II) is Gross Output; where $GO = GDP + II$. In terms of the Hayekian triangle, if GDP tracks vertical up and down movements, GO tracks left and right movements on the horizontal axis (this is not totally accurate, since GDP is included in GO). GO is important because business cycles are not only about GDP movements, they are also about inefficiencies and misallocation of resources in intermediate stages of production as well. GDP is blind to misallocation in the structure of production. If we are only concerned with what happens to the vertical axis, then we risk overlooking whether *how* GDP is achieved is stable in the first place (horizontal axis).

The allocation of time in the production process is defined by the interest rate. Therefore, if the monetary authority manages to keep *MV* stable, then the market interest rate does not deviate from the natural or equilibrium interest rate, avoiding business cycles of the Austrian type, which builds on deviations from (Wicksell, 1898) natural interest rate. It is for this reason that Hayek (1931, pp. 23–24) denominates as neutral the monetary policy that keeps *MV* stable maintaining the market interest rate at its natural level rather than referring to money neutrality as changes in money supply not affecting the price level (or relative prices) in the long-run. This is also why Hayek talks about neutral *policy* rather than neutral *money*. For the Hayek of *Prices and Production*, what should be targeted is the monetary policy that keeps the interest rate at its equilibrium level rather than focusing on the price level.

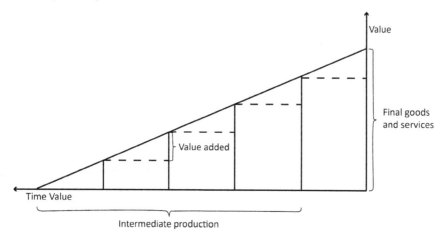

Figure 4.2 Hayekian triangle.

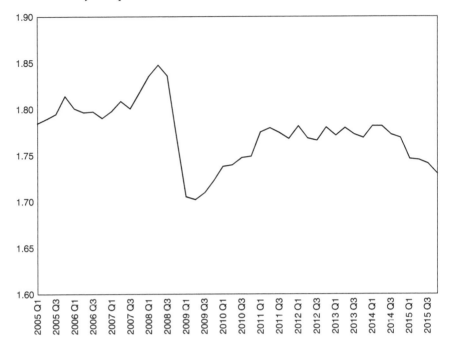

Figure 4.3 GO/GDP, United States, 2005–2015.

Source: Bureau of Economic Analysis.

Figure 4.3 shows the GO/GDP ratio (not seasonally adjusted) for the United States. During the 2008 crisis, the ratio falls from 1.85 to 1.70, and a downward movement can also be seen starting in late 2014. The percent fall of GO during the crisis is significantly larger than the fall of GDP. The yearly falls for the 2008 Q4–2009 Q3 period are −0.9%, −1.9%, −3.2%, and −3.1% for GDP; −3.6%, −8.9%, −10.8%, and −9.8% for GO. The fall in ratio at the end of the series is due to a relative deacceleration of GO between 2014 Q4 and 2015 Q4.

Even though good statistics for gross output or another estimate for all transactions taking place in the economy are rarely available, this is not the only series that can be used to diagnose if the chosen target on NGDP implies a loose monetary policy.

Final and intermediate prices

All else being equal, in a closed economy an increase in money supply produces an increase in the price level of final goods (a fall in the price of money). But in the real world, all else rarely remains constant. It is possible then, that inflation numbers depict an inaccurate stance of the monetary policy in place. As Selgin (1996, Chapter 7; 1997) points out, it is conceivable that the effect of an excess of money supply is offset by an increase in productivity. In a time-series graph, under monetary equilibrium the price level of final goods should fall at the rate of productivity or total factor productivity (TFP) gains. A plot that shows a flat line can give the wrong impression that monetary policy is on track rather than being too loose.

As was discussed in the second chapter, to target a nominal income variable such as NGDP is an indirect way of targeting the income of the factors of production. This is why under a nominal income regime a change in productivity produces a change in the price level of final goods. When there is a change in productivity, either the price of final goods falls or the price of factors of production increases. In terms of menu costs, the former is more efficient (Chapter 2). In other words, in the case of an excess of money supply in the presence of productivity gains, inflation (understood as an increase in the price level) is moved away from final prices and placed into intermediate prices. It follows, then, that a proxy to see if there is an excess of money supply in the presence of a stable final price level is to observe the behavior of a producer price index (PPI) with respect to a consumer price index (CPI).

This scenario where inflation is concealed behind productivity gains is not rare. In fact, it has been argued that there were significant productivity gains after the year 2000 (Gordon, 2010, pp. 8–10; Jorgenson, Ho, and Stiroh, 2008; Oliner, Sichel, and Stiroh, 2007; Selgin, Beckworth, and Bahadir, 2015). This means that the particular case where low inflation is consistent with a loose monetary policy is present in the years prior to the 2008 crisis. Figure 4.4 shows the U.S. CPI and PPI for the 1985–2016 period. The graph shows that since 2002 the PPI grows at

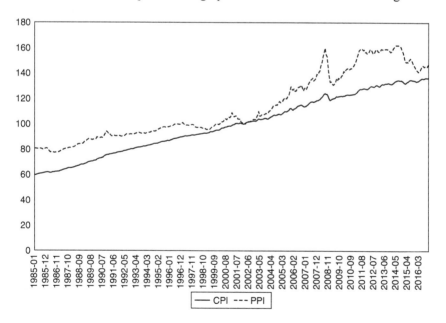

Figure 4.4 CPI and PPI, United States, 1985–2016, Jan 2002 = 100.

Source: U.S. Bureau of Labor Statistics, Consumer Price Index for All Urban Consumers: All Items and Producer Price Index for All Commodities.

a higher rate than the CPI, this suggests the presence of implicit inflation due to a loose monetary policy that started early in the 2000s.

Between December 2002 and December 2007, CPI and PPI grew at an average yearly rate of 3.0% and 5.8% respectively. Figure 4.4 is consistent with changes in TFP. (Selgin et al., 2015) estimate what the United States' Federal funds rate should have been if changes in productivity were taken into account; they also calculate the gap between the neutral and actual Federal funds rate (the "Productivity Gap"). They find that monetary policy was too loose between 2001 and 2006. This period of loose monetary policy also coincides with Taylor's (2009) analysis.[2] In a nutshell, the neutral Federal funds rate is a function of the time preference or discount rate, productivity growth, and labor input growth. This simple formula in fact shows how challenging it can be to carry on a neutral monetary policy given how difficult it can be to obtain good quality, real-time information of the required variables.

Upward movements in PPI may not only tell in advance that CPI inflation is likely to be happening in the future, they can also point to the presence of monetary disequilibrium even if CPI does not accelerate its growth rate.

Inflation not captured in price indices

There are some situations where an excess of money supply does not translate into an increase in the price level, or at least this effect gets significantly delayed making the behavior of the price level a loose indicator of whether or not monetary policy is on a good track. This is not to deny that an excess of money supply over money demand has no effect on the price level, but rather that beside significant lags, the way price levels are measured may leave loopholes through which inflation sneaks out. It is not enough, then, to look at the price level as the only diagnosis of a monetary disequilibrium in the form of an excess of money supply.[3]

One of these scenarios is pointed out by Leijonhufvud (2007; 2009) and W. R. White (2006), who argue that in a context of open economies, the price level is a loose indicator of monetary equilibrium since an excess of money supply can produce the alternative effect of an increase in imports. Consider a small, open economy with a fixed exchange rate. An excess of money supply over money demand results in an increase in consumption by economic agents. Unless domestic output also rises, this surge in consumption and investment is satisfied with an increase in imports. Since this is a small economy, the increase in consumption does not have a discernible effect on international prices. Domestic producers cannot increase their prices above their international competitors due to their consumer's small part of the world market. Certainly, non-tradable goods may see their prices increase, but it is possible that this has a delayed or too small an effect on the price level for monetary authorities to *see* inflation in the domestic economy. In addition, discerning between the tradable and non-tradable component of a price is not an easy task. A more attentive and perceptive monetary authority would consider a persistent trade deficit (in a small open economy with a fixed or regulated exchange rate) as a sign of potential excess of money supply. In other words, how an excess of money supply manifests in the economy depends on the institutional framework under which monetary policy is executed. Leijonhufvud and W. R. White claim that it was an effect similar to this one that made the price level be a loose indicator and misled central bankers on the stance of their monetary policy. The difference is that even though the United States is not a small economy, other major central banks kept their currencies depreciated vis-à-vis the Federal Reserve's expansionary policy to keep their exports flowing to the United States. Price level inflation in the United States failed to show higher levels of inflation as consumers in the United States imported goods from the rest of the world delaying the rise (increase) in domestic measures of inflation. But the stable price level observed in the United States paralleled a persistent trade deficit. This persistent trade deficit, however, was not diagnosed as the outcome of a loose monetary policy started by the Federal Reserve being mimicked by other major central banks.

Another reason why observing the price level may fail to alert about a loose monetary policy is because the prices being affected fall outside the prices included in the observed price level. An example of this situation is the price of houses in the United States. While the cost of *living* in a house, such as a rent, is included in the CPI, the price of *buying* a house is not. This means that if an excess of money supply is channeled through policy toward the housing market, the CPI will fail to show inflation as a sign of monetary policy being too loose early enough. The shortcoming of CPI is that it looks at *some* prices instead of looking at *all* prices in the economy. This would not be a serious issue if an excess of money supply affects all or most of the prices in the economy, but this issue can become significant when a policy in place channels the newly created money toward a good whose price is not included in CPI (more about this issue in Chapter 6).

To avoid this shortcoming, a policy maker may follow the inflation of the GDP deflator. Since GDP is observing all final goods and services, the GDP deflator is tracking the evolution of all final prices. Even if the GDP deflator improves the coverage offered by CPI, it can still present some loopholes through which symptoms of inflation are lost. For instance, the excess of money supply may be used to increase the purchases of durable goods that were not produced in the current year and therefore will not be included in the GDP deflator. Again, houses provide an example of this situation. The increase in the price of houses built in previous years will not be captured in the GDP deflator. Yet another case is the purchase of assets that are not supposed to be in GDP because they do not represent production of *new* goods. This is the case of stocks (change of ownership) and bonds (credits or loans). Similar to the above discussion with houses, an increase of money supply channeled toward the stock exchange can produce an increase in the price of financial assets, but not in CPI or the GDP deflator soon enough. However, monetary equilibrium depends on all transactions, not only on the transactions of newly created goods (intermediate or final). These situations can produce either a housing bubble or a financial bubble.[4] Bubbles are dangerous because they are hard to spot in their early stages. In a healthy and growing economy, it is expected for the price of stocks to increase as firms in the economy also increase their value. Therefore, observing an increasing value of the stock exchange does not necessarily mean monetary policy is off track any more than the economy is striving and that the chosen monetary policy is the right one. Bubbles become an evident issue once their sizes are too large to be ignored. Looking for bubbles is a challenging strategy to diagnose the stance of monetary policy.

From the above discussion, it follows there are serious challenges on the execution of monetary policy. For the monetary authority, the absence of inflation is no guarantee that monetary policy is on the right track and should not be interpreted as a green light to continue with their actual monetary policy. However, while the presence of inflation (deflation) may signal an excess (shortage) of money supply, it is also the case that the observed behavior might be the result of changes in productivity and not due to a monetary disequilibrium or policy mistake.[5] In particular, the presence of deflation should not be immediately taken as the presence of a crisis or a depression. As was mentioned in the previous chapter, in terms of an aggregate demand and aggregate supply model, a depression is captured by a left movement on the horizontal axis (output), not in a downward movement on the vertical axis (consumer price level). Increases in productivity produce good or benign deflation which should not be confused with a fall in aggregate demand (bad or malign deflation).[6]

The effect of monetary disequilibrium in the time allocation of the production process

There is still another way to analyze the stance of the monetary policy in place. To the extent that central banks channel changes in money supply through the financial market, interest rates will be affected first. This is because the central bank is not just changing the supply of money; it is doing so by changing the supply of credit. As the supply of credit increases (decreases) its price will fall (rise). If the central bank were to expand (contract) money supply by buying (selling) goods, then the direct effect would be on the price level rather than on interest rates. In fact, it is not out of the ordinary for central banks to target an interest rate as the Federal Reserve does with the Federal funds rate. Therefore, if the monetary policy is expansionary (tight) the targeted interest rate will be below (above) its natural or equilibrium level.

It should be clarified that the equilibrium rate of interest is not any interest rate at which there is full employment. The equilibrium rate of interest is the specific interest rate at which the time allocation of resources is correctly distributed across the process of production. On one hand, the low interest rate incentivizes investment and consumption, increasing employment. On the other hand, since interest rate is the price of time, by being below its equilibrium level producers want to use more time than consumers are willing to wait by postponing consumption. Intuitively, the time it takes to produce goods is neither too long nor too short. A monetary policy that locates the interest rate below its equilibrium level may achieve full employment and a "shortage of time." This time misallocation eventually proves to be costly. As an equilibrium value, the natural rate of interest

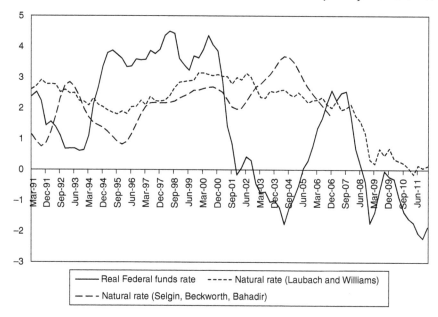

Figure 4.5 Federal funds rate and estimations of the natural rate of interest.

is unknown and non-observable. The natural rate of interest as a benchmark of monetary policy is further complicated by the fact that there is not a unique inter-est rate, but different rates for different maturity dates. This means that ideally the monetary authority should keep the whole yield curve at its natural level and slope. Laubach and Williams (2003) and Selgin et al. (2015) offer estimations of the natural rate of interest the Federal Reserve should target. Figure 4.5 shows both natural rates of interest next to the actual real Federal funds rate.[7] These esti-mations suggest that the Federal Reserve led the Federal funds rate to go below its equilibrium or natural level between 2001 and 2005.[8]

For Laubach and Williams (2003) the natural rate of interest has two compo-nents, the growth rate of the real GDP trend and "other determinants" such as household's rate of time preference. Selgin et al. (2015) offer a similar relation, but they disaggregate the growth in output in two drivers, productivity gains and increases in labor. In their model the natural rate of interest depends on the time preference, productivity growth, and labor input growth. This allows them to iso-late the direct effect that changes on TFP have on the natural interest rate. Selgin et al. (2015) argue that the surge in TFP that started in the 1990s mislead the monetary authorities in the years prior to the 2008 crisis. These two series suggest that during the 1990s the Federal Reserve was somewhat tight, but that its policy becomes quite loose in late 2001 even producing a negative real Federal funds rate starting in early 2003.

The problems caused by an interest rate outside equilibrium are difficult to diagnose because they do not show up in the usual way policy makers evaluate the stance of monetary policy. Low and stable inflation and full employment are consistent with an interest rate outside its equilibrium level. The fact that the natural rate of equilibrium (all else equal) yields a low and stable inflation and full employment does not mean that if we observe low and stable inflation and full employment the interest rate is at its equilibrium level.

Even though the intuition of the effects produced by movements in the interest rate is straightforward, its theoretical representation and empirical observation is filled with challenges.[9] If the relative price of time decreases (increases), then we should expect the "consumption" of time to increase (decrease).[10] But what it means to "consume" time and how time in the production process should be measured are very difficult tasks that led to several capital controversies in the late 19th century and in the 20th century as well.[11] The concept of *time* and present value *sensitivity* to movements in interest rates is captured in the financial concept of *duration*. While Macaulay duration offers a measure of the weighted average life of a cash-flow, modified duration is a measurement of the present value sensitivity to changes in the discount rate. These two measures (Macaulay duration and modified duration), which are equal when time is modeled as a continuous variable, capture in a well-defined formula the two concepts behind the Austrian concept of *roundaboutness*. One, that the present value of longer investment projects is more sensitive than shorter investment projects to changes in the discount rate. Two, that the present value of more capital intense projects is more sensitive than less capital intense projects to changes in the discount rate. Even if we assume that changes in money supply do not affect relative prices of goods and inputs, monetary policy can have an effect on the relative present value of different investment projects. It is the relative change in present values that triggers a reallocation of resources.

To the extent that monetary policy has an effect on the discount rate used by investors to value potential investment projects, then the effect of a monetary policy on the present value of these projects is uneven. A downward movement of the discount rate makes all present values increase, but the longer and larger projects (in terms of financial capital) increase more in relative terms than shorter and small projects. In relative terms, projects that require more time and financial capital increase their value and climb the ranking of projects in the eyes of the investors when the central bank carries a policy that reduces the interest rates on the market. This familiar *duration* effect is the core and distinctive characteristic of the ABCT; which relies on imbalances produced in the allocation of resources *across* time. In short, the ABCT relies on the change of relative prices of investment projects (present values) as captured in financial analysis. Inversely, an upward movement of the discount rate makes all present values fall, but those of longer and larger projects fall more in relative terms. Now the longer and larger projects fall in their ranking and they may become unprofitable. This zig zag movement on relative present values of different projects sends price signals, first to allocate resources on long and large projects and then to reallocate them in shorter and small projects. This allocation and reallocation of resources is costly due to the irreversibility of investment and to physical and human capital heterogeneity, a distinctive feature in the Austrian literature.[12]

This discussion on deviations from the natural rate of interest point out two important features. First, that full employment is no guarantee that the economy is in equilibrium because there can be disequilibrium in *how* factors of production under full employment are allocated across time. Second, given a crisis, a low interest rate policy intended to trigger an economic recovery can increase output and employment but at the expense of producing an unsustainable allocation of resources due to the interest rate being located out of its equilibrium level. *How* goods are produced is as important as *what* is being produced. Economic stability it not only a matter of quantity of output, it is also about how resources are combined and allocated. If we were to picture this situation in a production possibilities frontier (PPF) graph, a crisis would make the economy to fall inside the PPF, but a monetary-policy-driven economic recovery occurs under the short-term monetary effects on relative prices and present values. This means that even though the economy may approach its PPF (full employment), it will do so at the wrong point or combination of goods. If this allocation of resources is unprofitable, then the monetary stimulus cannot be discontinued without producing a new fall in the level of output.

A financial framework of monetary policy effects and ABCT[13]

The discussed effects of monetary policy on the allocation of resources can be framed in the same financial terms used by investors to value their portfolio of projects. Consider the present value (*PV*) calculation of a free-cash-flow (*FCF*) with *T* periods discounted at the cost of opportunity rate (*c*) (for simplicity it is assumed that the discount rate is constant on time).

$$PV = \sum_{t=0}^{T} \frac{FCF_t}{(1+c)^t} \tag{4.1}$$

where the free-cash-flow equals the net operating profits after taxes (*NOPAT*) minus the net investment (*NI*) of the period; $FCF_t = NOPAT_t - NI_t$. Since the net investment is the change in the (financial) capital of the firm, the *FCF* representation can be algebraically transformed into its EVA® representation.[14]

$$PV = K_0 + \sum_{t=1}^{T} \frac{(ROIC_t - c)K_{t-1}}{(1+c)^t} = K_0 + \sum_{t=1}^{T} \frac{EVA_t}{(1+c)^t} = K_0 + MVA_t \tag{4.2}$$

where *ROIC* represents the *return over invested capital*, *EVA* is the economic profits, and *MVA* shows the market value added *to* today's market prices of the capital owned by the firm. The EVA® representation of the *FCF* approach is useful because it brings to surface a variable for capital. Two effects can then be shown. First, that two cash-flows with the same *K* but different *T* have a different duration, where the cash-flow with a larger *T* has the larger *duration*. This means longer cash-flows have a larger average period of production and also that the *PV* of the longer cash-flow is more sensitive or elastic to changes in the discount rate or cost of opportunity. Second, that two cash-flows with the same *T* but different *K* also have a different *duration*. The cash-flow with the larger *K* has the larger *duration*. This means that the *PV* of projects that require more (financial) capital are also more sensitive or elastic to changes in the discount rate or cost of opportunity (N. Cachanosky and Lewin, 2014). The Macaulay duration is represented in Equation 4.3.

$$D = \frac{\sum_{t=1}^{T} (EVA_t \cdot t)/(1+c)^t}{MVA} \tag{4.3}$$

The first effect, that longer cash-flows have larger durations, is a well-known situation in the finance literature. The second effect, that larger projects have larger duration comes to the surface once the *FCF* is transformed into its *EVA* equivalent. These formulas give mathematical consistency to the theoretical core of the ABCT and the effects of monetary policy on how resources are allocated across time. Since duration values differ across projects with different time horizons or required financial investment, the present value of a *high roundabout* (*HR*) and a *low roundabout* (*LR*) project changes with movements in the discount rate in a specific direction. More precisely, *c* and PV_{HR}/PV_{LR} are negatively correlated in a measureable and tractable way.[15] As PV_{HR}/PV_{LR} increases, when interest rates are moved downward by the monetary authority, marginal investment takes place in projects that are too long or require too much capital. But at the natural or equilibrium interest rate, this project can either be less profitable than the investor was expecting it to be or even make losses (the EVAs or economic profits are less than the cost of opportunity and the MVA is negative).

It is not eccentric to consider, then, that an expansionary monetary policy aimed at stimulating the economy will do so by fostering projects which are too long or too large and not sustainable at the equilibrium interest rate. This distinction, however, does not show up in standard macroeoconomic aggregates such as GDP and its components.

Notes

1 Several scholars, for instance, have turned to the Austrian Business Cycle Theory (ABCT) to have a more complete explanation of how and why the 2008 crisis happened (Calvo, 2013; Hume and Sentance, 2009; Leijonhufvud, 2009). For a discussion on the renewed interest on the ABCT see N. Cachanosky and Salter (2017).
2 Selgin et al.'s (2015) analysis also finds a period of loose monetary policy during the 1970s, similar to a Taylor's rule result for such period.
3 This issue relates to a topic previously discussed if inflation should be understood in its traditional meaning as an excess of money supply or as an increase in the price level. These two definitions are not just two sides of the same coin. If inflation is to be understood just as an increase in the price level, then it is possible that an observed stable price level occurs while there is an excess of money supply. At least in the short run, an increase In the price level is one of the possible symptoms of an excess of

money supply. Besides the previously discussed case of implicit inflation, an increase in imports is another potential symptom.

4 Anderson (1949), and J. C. Cachanosky (1989) argue that this is what triggered the financial bubble that burst in the crisis of 1929. The Federal Reserve was channeling its expansionary monetary policy of the 1920s through brokers that would acquire financial assets. These transactions would not be reflected as higher inflation rates. This situation reversed when the Federal Reserve decided to cut back on their policy; not because of inflation, but because of the financial bubble.

5 According to Selgin (1997, p. 49), theoretical "arguments favouring a productivity norm run counter to macro-economic conventional wisdom in a number of obvious ways. They suggest that a falling price level is not necessarily a sign or source of depression, that a rising price level is not necessarily a sign of excessive monetary expansion nor a justification for monetary tightening, and that a stable price level is not necessarily conducive to macro-economic stability. Modern economic history is filled with episodes supporting each of these claims, while contradicting conventional thinking as embodied in arguments for zero inflation." Selgin continues to support his argument by discussing some historical cases that defy the "macro-economic conventional wisdom."

6 It can be granted that a policy maker has better real-time information of the vertical axis (prices levels) than the horizontal axis (output) and that this is why policy makers rely so much on this variable. Still, this difference in how fast reliable information is available does not mean that a fall in the price level implies a fall in output. This may or may not be the case.

This argument, however, does not hold in the field of economic history, where the economic historian should be able to look at output variables to diagnose whether or not there was an economic crisis at any point in time rather than looking at the price level. For some historical cases see Selgin (1997, Chapter IV).

7 The real Federal funds rate is estimated by subtracting the nominal rate from the yearly inflation rate.

8 I thank George Selgin and David Beckworth for providing the calculations.

9 For empirical studies that follow Garrison (2001) see Luther and Cohen (2014), Mulligan (2002; 2013), and A. T. Young (2005; 2012; 2015). Also see L. H. White (2012, Chapter 3).

10 For a discussion about time as a factor of production, see Kirzner (2010, Chapter 3).

11 For a review of the capital controversies, see Cohen (2008; 2010), Cohen and Harcourt (2003), Felipe and Fisher (2003), Felipe and McCombie (2014), and Yeager, (1976). For discussion on the average period of production see Hayek (1935), Knight (1935), and Machlup (1935).

12 On investment irreversible see Dixit and Pyndick (1994). On capital heterogeneity and theory see Horwitz (2000, Chapter 2), Kirzner (2010), Lachmann (1956; 1977), Lewin (1999), and Powell (2010).

13 For a more detailed discussion of this section see N. Cachanosky (2015), N. Cachanosky and Lewin (2014, 2016b), and Lewin and Cachanosky (2016; 2017). This duration effect discussed in this section is already embedded in Garrison's (2001) treatment of Hayek (1931). Hayek's triangle offers a special case of duration. In the Garrison–Hayek treatment the average period of production is in the middle of the horizontal axis that tracks time-value; this special case of duration as half of the life of the cash-flow occurs when a simple (non-compounding) interest rate is assumed just as Hayek's triangle does. For another application of the concept of duration see Hendrickson and Salter (2016) and Osborne and Davidson (2016).

14 For a step-by-step derivation see N. Cachanosky and Lewin (2014, p. 663), and Koller, Goedhart, and Wessels (1990, pp. 697–699). On EVA® see Ehrbar (1998), Stern, Shiely, and Ross (2003), D. S. Young and O'Byrne (2000).

15 For an empirical application see N. Cachanosky and Lewin (2016a).

References

Anderson, B. M. (1949). *Economics and the Public Welfare* (1980 ed.). Indianapolis: Liberty Fund.

Cachanosky, J. C. (1989). La Crisis del Treinta. *Libertas*, 10.(Mayo).

Cachanosky, N. (2015). Expectation in Austrian Business Cycle Theory: Market Share Matters. *The Review of Austrian Economics*, 28.(2): 151–165.

Cachanosky, N., and Lewin, P. (2014). Roundaboutness Is Not a Mysterious Concept: A Financial Application to Capital Theory. *Review of Political Economy*, 26.(4): 648–665.

Cachanosky, N., and Lewin, P. (2016a). An Empirical Application of the EVA® Framework to Business Cycles. *Review of Financial Economics*, 30.(September): 60–67.

Cachanosky, N., and Lewin, P. (2016b). Financial Foundations of Austrian Business Cycle Theory. *Advances in Austrian Economics*, 20: 15–44.

Cachanosky, N., and Salter, A. W. (2017). The View from Vienna: An Analysis of the Renewed Interest in the Mises–Hayek Theory of the Business Cycle. *The Review of Austrian Economics*, 30.(2): 169–192.

Calvo, G. A. (2013). Puzzling Over the Anatomy of Crises: Liquidity and the Veil of Finance. *Monetary and Economic Studies*, (November): 39–63.

Cohen, A. J. (2008). The Mythology of Capital or of Static Equilibrium? The Böhm-Bawerk/Clark Controversy. *Journal of the History of Economic Thought*, 30.(2): 151–171.

Cohen, A. J. (2010). Capital Controverisy from Bohm-Bawerk to Bliss: Badly Posed or Very Deep Questions? Or What "We" Can Learn from Capital Controversy Even If We Don't Care Who Won. *Journal of the History of Economic Thought*, 32.(1): 1–21.

Cohen, A. J., and Harcourt, G. C. (2003). Whatever Happened to the Cambridge Capital Theory Controversies? Preliminaries: Joan Robinson's Complaints. *Journal of Economic Perspectives*, 17.(1): 199–214.

Dixit, A. K., and Pyndick, R. S. (1994). *Irreversible Investment*. Princeton: Princeton University Press.

Ehrbar, A. (1998). *EVA: The Real Key to Creating Wealth*. Hoboken: Wiley Publishers.

Felipe, J., and Fisher, F. M. (2003). Aggregation in Production Functions: What Applied Economists Should Know. *Metroeconomica*, 54.(2): 208–262.

Felipe, J., and McCombie, J. S. L. (2014). The Aggregate Production Function: "Not Even Wrong." *Review of Political Economy*, 26.(1): 60–84.

Garrison, R. W. (2001). *Time and Money. The Macroeconomics of Capital Structure* (2002 ed.). London and New York: Routledge.

Gordon, R. J. (2010). Revisiting U.S. Productivity Growth Over the Past Century with a View of the Future. *NBER Working Paper No. 15834*. Cambridge: NBER.

Hayek, F. A. (1931). *Prices and Production* (1967 ed.). New York: Augustus M. Kelley.

Hayek, F. A. (1935). The Maintenance of Capital. *Economica*, 2.(7): 241–276.

Hendrickson, J. R., and Salter, A. W. (2016). Money, Liquidity, and the Structure of Production. *Journal of Economic Dynamics and Control*, 73: 314–328.

Horwitz, S. G. (2000). *Microfoundations and Macroeconomics: An Austrian Perspective* (2003 ed.). London and New York: Routledge.

Hume, M., and Sentance, A. (2009). The Global Credit Boom: Challenges for Macroeconomics and Policy. *Journal of International Money and Finance*, 28.(8): 1426–1461.

Jorgenson, D. W., Ho, M. S., and Stiroh, K. J. (2008). A Retrospective Look at the U.S. Productivity Growth Resurgence. *Journal of Economic Perspectives*, 22.(1): 3–24.

Kirzner, I. M. (2010). *Essays on Capital and Interest*. Indianapolis: Liberty Fund.

Knight, F. H. (1935). Professor Hayek and the Theory of Investment. *The Economic Journal*, 45.(177): 77–94.

Koller, T., Goedhart, M., and Wessels, D. (1990). *Valuation: Measuring and Managing the Value of Companies* (2010 ed.). Hoboken: Wiley.

Lachmann, L. M. (1956). *Capital and Its Structure* (1978 ed.). Kansas City: Sheed Andrews and McMeel.

Lachmann, L. M. (1977). *Capital, Expectations, and the Market Process.* Kansas City: Sheed Andrews and McMeel.

Laubach, T., and Williams, J. (2003). Measuring the Natural Rate of Interest. *The Review of Economics and Statistics*, 85.(4): 1063–1070.

Leijonhufvud, A. (2007). Monetary and Financial Stability. *Policy Insight No. 14*. London: Centre for Economic Policy Research.

Leijonhufvud, A. (2009). Out of the Corridor: Keynes and the Crisis. *Cambridge Journal of Economics*, 33.(4): 741–757.

Lewin, P. (1999). *Capital in Disequilibrium* (2011 ed.). Auburn: Ludwig von Mises Institute.

Lewin, P., and Cachanosky, N. (2016). A Financial Framework for Understanding Macroeconomic Cycles. *Journal of Financial Economic Policy*, 8.(2): 268–280.

Lewin, P., and Cachanosky, N. (2017). Value and Capital: Austrian Capital Theory, Retrospect and Prospect. *The Review of Austrian Economics*, 31.(1): 1–26. https://doi.org/10.1007/s11138-016-0374-8.

Luther, W. J., and Cohen, M. (2014). An Empirical Analysis of the Austrian Business Cycle Theory. *Atlantic Economic Journal*, 42.(2): 153–169.

Machlup, F. (1935). Professor Knight and the Period of Production. *The Journal of Political Economy*, 43.(5): 577–624.

Mulligan, R. F. (2002). A Hayekian Analysis of the Structure of Production. *Quarterly Journal of Austrian Economics*, 5.(2): 17–33.

Mulligan, R. F. (2013). New Evidence on the Structure of Production: Real and Austrian Business Cycle Theory and the Financial Instability Hypothesis. *Journal of Economic Behavior and Organization*, 86: 67–77.

Oliner, S. D., Sichel, D. E., and Stiroh, K. J. (2007). Explaining a Productive Decade. *Brookings Papers on Economic Activity*, 2007.(1): 81–137.

Osborne, M., and Davidson, I. (2016). The Cambridge Capital Controversies: Contributions from the Complex Plane. *Review of Political Economy*, 28.(2): 251–269.

Powell, B. (2010). Some Implications of Capital Heterogeneity. In P. J. Boettke (Ed.), *Handbook on Contemporary Austrian Economics* (pp. 124–135). Cheltenham and Northampton: Edward Elgar.

Selgin, G. A. (1996 [2002]). *Bank Deregulation and Monetary Order*. New York: Routledge.

Selgin, G. A. (1997). *Less Than Zero*. London: The Institute of Economic Affairs.

Selgin, G. A., Beckworth, D., and Bahadir, B. (2015). The Productivity Gap: Monetary Policy, the Subprime Boom, and the Post-2001 Productivity Surge. *Journal of Policy Modeling*, 37.(2): 189–207.

Stern, J. M., Shiely, J. S., and Ross, I. (2003). *The EVA Challenge*. New York: Wiley.

Taylor, J. B. (2009). *Getting Off Track*. Stanford: Hoover Institute Press.

White, L. H. (2012). *The Clash of Economic Ideas*. Cambridge: Cambridge University Press.

White, W. R. (2006). Is Price Stability Enough? *BIS Working Papers No. 205*. Basel: Bank for International Settlements.

Wicksell, K. (1898). *Interest and Prices* (1962 ed.). New York: Sextry Press.

Yeager, L. B. (1976). Toward Understanding Some Paradoxes in Capital-theory. *Economic Inquiry*, 14.(3): 313–346.

Young, A. T. (2005). Reallocating Labor to Initiate Changes in Capital Structures: Hayek Revisited. *Economics Letters*, 89.(3): 275–282.

Young, A. T. (2012). The Time Structure of Production in the US, 2002–2009. *The Review of Austrian Economics*, 25.(2): 77–92.

Young, A. T. (2015). Austrian Business Cycle Theory: A Modern Appraisal. In P. J. Boettke and C. J. Coyne (Eds), *Oxford Handbook of Austrian Economics*. Oxford: Oxford University Press.

Young, D. S., and O'Byrne, S. E. (2000). *EVA and Value-Based Management*. New York: McGraw-Hill.

5 Nominal income targeting as market outcome versus policy outcome

Introduction

Previous chapters argue about the convenience of stabilizing a nominal income variable, such as NGDP. Further, this policy maintains the benefits of other policies or rules with the enhancement that it allows real shocks to be separated from nominal shocks. However, achieving the right level and behavior of NGDP is not the only important issue a central bank has to deal with. It is not just the level of NGDP that matters, but also its composition. In particular what real GDP looks like and how resources are allocated. A certain level and behavior of NGDP can be achieved either as a policy outcome under the presence of a central bank, or as a market outcome, which would be the case in a free-banking scenario. Both values of NGDP may have a different real composition. As long as we believe that the micro composition of the macro variables does matter, then to consider *how* NGDP is created is also an important issue. If that is the case, then central banks need to also consider their limits in achieving microeconomic equilibrium from macroeconomic equilibrium.

This chapter is divided in four sections. The first one compares how NGDP is created under free banking and under central banking. The second one deals with Hayek's knowledge problem in the realm of monetary policy. The third section discusses the Cantillon Effect that occurs when new money enters the economy through different entry points. The last section discusses the possibility of a constitutional monetary policy; a policy rule that is beyond the control of the policy makers assigned to execute it in the first place.

NGDP value versus NGDP composition

In the case of free banking, the supply of commodity money (i.e. gold) is an *endogenous* outcome of the market process. Commercial banks receive deposits in gold and issue convertible banknotes that are used as a money substitute by economic agents. Both the production of gold and issuance of convertible banknotes are market decisions, not the result of policy given to the market. Recall Equation 2.4 which offers a slightly modified equation of exchange where money supply (M) is opened into gold (G) and the money multiplier (m) effect.

$$G \cdot m \cdot V_Y = P_Y \cdot Y \tag{2.4}$$

Assume for simplicity that all units of gold are held as deposits and that economic agents use convertible banknotes in their transactions. In this scenario, both G and m are *endogenous* variables. The supply of base money differs in two ways between free banking (commodity money) and central banking (fiat money). First, under free banking there are multiple miners on the supply side of the market of gold, while under central banking there is one government monopolist. Second, under free banking the supply of gold is driven by maximization of the miner's profits as in any other industry, while under central banking, profit and loss calculation is not a leading factor of monetary policy.[1] Gold suppliers in free banking will only incur the cost of mining gold if they expect to receive at least a normal rate of profit. Therefore, if the supply of gold is such that its purchasing power is not high enough to mine more gold, the supply of gold will not increase.[2]

Because issuer banks in free banking are profit-maximizing firms (given their desired level of reserves), the value of the money multipliers is also an endogenous variable. It is possible that the supply of gold might not be elastic enough to accommodate to changes in money demand. This "elasticity gap" between money demand and money supply is filled by the issuance of banknotes. As money demand increases banks, see the level of reserves rising above their desired level. When this occurs, commercial banks expand the circulation of their convertible banknotes dropping the reserve ratio back to their desired level. It is this behavior that keeps GmV stable. Therefore, an increase in the demand for money can be accommodated by an increase in the supply of money substitutes rather than base money. There are three interacting pieces to consider. First, changes to the supply of money. Second, changes in money demand. Third, how changes in money demand are going to be accommodated through changes in money supply. Under free banking, all these three pieces are *endogenous* or market driven.

But this is not the case anymore under a central banking regime. Because under central banking the endogeneity of money supply is broken, it is now up to policy makers to achieve monetary equilibrium. In the absence of a complete market of money, the required market information for monetary equilibrium is also lacking. Therefore, policy makers need to use a proxy of monetary equilibrium as their benchmark. As was discussed with the case of the price level, choosing the wrong benchmark can mislead policy makers. Consider now the case of central banking represented in Equation 5.1. In this equation gold is replaced by the central bank's fiat money (F).

$$F \cdot m \cdot V_Y = P_Y \cdot Y \tag{5.1}$$

There are two important changes in this equation with respect to Equation 2.4. The first and most obvious one, is that of replacing gold with fiat money. The supply of fiat money does not only come from the central bank as the sole supplier, but its supply is not driven by profit maximization, as is the case of gold miners (and the production cost of fiat money is virtually zero). The second important difference is on the money multiplier. Under central banking, commercial banks do not issue liabilities in the form of convertible banknotes as they would under free banking. In a free-banking regime, if there is an excessive increase of money supply in the form of convertible banknotes, banks see reserves fall below their desired level and reduce their circulating banknotes accordingly. But when banks receive newly created fiat money they treat the increase in reserves similarly to an increase in money demand under free banking rather than as an excess of banknotes in circulation. In short, the signals of an excess of money supply (i.e. adverse clearing) are looser and more erratic under central banking than under free banking. Central banks cannot rely on the secondary creation of money as a market process that contributes to monetary equilibrium because the market signals work differently than under free banking.

Consider now the dynamics of each monetary regime. In the case of free banking there are several money injection points in the economy; each bank that issues convertible banknotes is a potential injection point (Salter, 2013). This means that free banking is more flexible in the sense of allowing changes in money supply to happen closer to the optimal injection point. On the contrary, in the case of central banking there is only one injection point, the central bank. At first sight, it might seem that there is no major difference between each case. After all, a central bank also channels an increase in money supply through the financial market. There are, however, three differences to consider.

The first one is that under free banking the injection points of money include *all* commercial banks, but under central banking it is usually with a smaller number of larger banks (primary dealers) – the ones that qualify to receive new reserves from the central bank.[3] This means that revenue from new credits tends to be more concentrated on larger banks under central banking than under free banking. Surely, these banks buy the reserves by selling treasury bonds or another financial asset and their balance sheets do not change their size. But as long as this exchange is voluntary, it reveals that these banks are better off with reserves than the financial assets they are giving up. As long as open market operations are voluntary, these are not zero-sum transactions. This means that banks that qualify to participate in the Federal Reserve's open market operations have an advantage over other banks. Second, even if for depositors all banks offer services that are perfect substitutes, they may still not behave similarly in the way they allocate credit. For a depositor, it may make no difference whether he holds a bank account with Bank A or Bank B. But these two banks may have different lending practices or may specialize in different industries. For instance, as of July 15, 2008, Lehman Brothers Inc. was one of the Federal Reserve primary dealers. Lehman's investment strategy proved to be unprofitable.[4] The third difference is that under free banking, where by definition there is no market regulation, each commercial bank runs a risk and profit analysis before issuing a loan to a business. But under central banking it is possible that certain regulations require banks to overlook risk and allocate credit to particular markets. For instance, there may be political reasons to channel credit to a particular sector of the economy such as mortgages to increase home ownership (discussed in the next chapter).

Central banks need, first, to know what monetary equilibrium looks like. A Keynesian framework points to consumer price level stability. But historical cases of free banking point to nominal income targeting. Second, central banks need to know how far off they are from monetary equilibrium and how to get to equilibrium. But information required for such a task is missing the mere existence of a central bank. Because of this, policy makers face a knowledge problem.

The knowledge problem and monetary policy

Hayek's (1948, Chapter IV) knowledge problem arises in the context of the socialist calculation debate in the first half of the 20th century. Even though Hayek's context is different to that of central banking, some of Hayek's arguments still have implications for monetary policy under central banking (Salter and Smith, 2017).[5] It should be noted that Hayek's point does not just rely on a shortage of calculating power by the central economic planner. The problem is not whether computers are powerful enough to store and use large quantities of data, but rather whether the required information exists and how it is going to be processed.[6]

The first issue to point out is that the information required to centrally organize an economy is not *given* to any particular individual and therefore is not out there waiting to be taken by central planners. Hayek argues that market information is dispersed in infinitely small bits through all the economic agents that participate in the economy. However, the issue is not just that information is dispersed as micro data across the whole economy, but that said information cannot exist *without* a market process in the first place. The reason for this is that it is the market process itself that generates the information. This is why information is dispersed as bits across all economic agents. Put differently, data such as prices and quantities are not an *input* to, but an *outcome* of, the market process. By eliminating private property rights and free exchanges between economic agents, the process that produces information ceases to work.[7] The information is not even dispersed in micro bits anymore, the information is just not there. This is why for Hayek assuming that information is given to economic agents is assuming the problem away, rather than offering an actual solution to the problem in hand. The central planner is in a very different position to that of the economist who builds an economic model. The central planner is working *inside* an unknown model, not building one.

The second issue is that there is a conceptual distinction to be made between *information* and *knowledge* (Zanotti, 2011). Information is a *quantitative* and *objective* concept, such as prices and quantities, and therefore it can be complete (perfect) or incomplete (imperfect). But *knowledge* is a *qualitative* and *subjective* concept, such as knowing how to ride a bike or run a business, and therefore can neither be complete nor incomplete (but it can be right or wrong, as would be falling from the bike or going through bankruptcy). This distinction is important because the same information can result in a different analysis due to different knowledge. For instance, the same information about the Great Depression can be given to a monetarist, a Keynesian, and an Austrian economist, but each one of them would *interpret* the information differently. The same data can tell different stories. Sometimes these stories may be complementary, but sometimes they may contradict each other. This distinction between information and knowledge means that having access to the former *is not sufficient* for the economy to reach equilibrium. More precisely, prices might well be necessary to have a well-functioning economy, but they are not sufficient. The information that prices provide needs to be correctly understood.[8]

Kirzner's (1973) contribution is to provide content to this knowledge problem, which takes the form of entrepreneurial *alertness*. This *alertness* is the distinctive ability of the entrepreneur *as* entrepreneur to discover market disequilibria that remain hidden to other entrepreneur's eyes. This *alertness* is the driving force behind the market convergence toward equilibrium. Without entrepreneurial *alertness*, reallocation of resources that would move the economy toward equilibrium would not take place. This is how Kirzner gives a more specific theoretical content to the role of Hayek's knowledge problem in the market process. Kirzner (1992, Chapter 10) also distinguishes between two types of knowledge problem. Knowledge problem A is the case of an over-optimism that results in an excess of supply. Since in this case economic profits are less than expected, this Type-A error is self-correcting. If the producer does not fix his overproduction he will eventually go bankrupt. Knowledge problem B is the case of unperceived profit opportunities. Error Type-B is not self-correcting and can remain undiscovered indefinitely.[9] For the economy to converge to equilibrium, both types of error should be corrected. But economic rationality, in the form of profit and loss analysis, can only solve errors of Type-A. To discover and remove errors of Type-B entrepreneurial *alertness* is needed. Note that this *alertness* is not just about predicting future events, but about discovering disequilibria when no one else does. An alternative way of framing Kirzner's argument is that the entrepreneurial *alertness* consists of the ability of going from the *unknown unknowns* to a *known unknown*. This is why in the Mises–Hayek–Kirzner argument the entrepreneur is the driving force of the market and it makes little sense to have a model of the economy where there are no entrepreneurs.

As mentioned before, even if Hayek's arguments take place in the context of the socialist calculation debate, some of their implications still hold for the problem of central banking. An important issue is that a central bank as a monopolist supplier of base money does not just supply an economic good, it supplies the economic good that is used as money in the whole economy. Following Selgin's (1988, pp. 89–94) example, assume there is a shoe producer who is a monopolist. Even if this monopolist does not face competition, it can still perform a profit and loss analysis of its business since he is facing market costs and his revenue is determined by market prices. The situation is different in the case of modern central banks that supply fiat money. A first difference is that the central bank faces virtually no production costs. A second difference is that the adverse clearing mechanism that keeps banks in check under free banking becomes significantly less reliable. Unlike the shoe monopolist, the central bank cannot rely on economic profit and loss analysis to optimize the supply of money. The economic rationale to optimize behavior becomes unreliable under central banking by its own existence and a substitute is required.

This situation raises two challenges to central banking. The first one is the need to find a good substitute for the equilibrium mechanism present under free banking that is absent under central banking. This can take the form of statistical analysis and model calibration as a substitute for profit maximization. Especially after the Keynesian revolution this substitution took place in the form of price level stability. The problem with this policy is that it does not guarantee monetary equilibrium, which should allow for a change in the price level inversely proportional to changes in productivity. Even if the substitute was nominal income stability, this choice would still require building the right variable in a timely manner while under free banking it is not even necessary to calculate nominal income in the first place. The central bank needs to be able to forecast the right level and trend of money demand, but under free banking this is achieved without the need of such a specific and challenging forecast. Under free banking, monetary equilibrium is a market outcome, not an objective that depends on the central bank expertise. Under free banking no one needs to produce a certain level of NGDP.

The second challenge is that a central bank is not subject to forces of market competition. As long as there is free entry and exit of firms, inefficient entrepreneurs are driven out of the market by more efficient entrepreneurs. Historical cases of free banking show that the same occurs under a competitive and free market of money and banking.[10] But if a central bank goes onto the wrong policy path, there is no clear market signal that would alert the policy maker about its mistake soon enough. This situation means that there is no market process to filter out the wrong models and monetary rules used by central bankers since the same data can be used to support different models at the same time. Recall that a crisis as big as that of 2008 happened without the standard signals, such as high inflation, alerting central bankers about a large disequilibrium. There was no clear sign that the dynamic stochastic general equilibrium models were sending monetary policy off track until it was too late. Furthermore, as discussed in the second chapter, for some advocates of NGDP Targeting the main problem of the 2008 crisis was the non-corrected fall in NGDP, not NGDP growing too fast in the years prior to the crisis. Policy makers face the particular challenge of not receiving confirmation that their policies are on the right track, and they are not always going to receive a clear sign when they are on the wrong path.

As long as there is a central bank, there is no such thing as not doing monetary policy and letting the market forces keep monetary equilibrium. This means that an efficient policy maker does not only need to master the required technical and scientific knowledge, already a challenge in itself, they also need to have the right Kirznerian *alertness* about the situation of the economy that data and technical knowledge does not provide. Monetary policy is not just a *technical* problem, it is also a *knowledge* or *alertness* issue. Central bankers need to be no less able to discover Type-B errors than entrepreneurs do in the market. Even more challenging, the policy maker's Kirznerian *alertness* needs to be superior to that of the average entrepreneur in the sense that by not doing policy under competitive market forces policy mistakes do not manifest as losses would do in any other industry. While in a competitive market a number of entrepreneurs compete to discover Type-B errors, under central banking we rely on the competence of only one institution. It is not implausible to consider that the central banking regime asks too much from policy makers.[11]

Central banks face still another challenge, that of being a Big Player (Koppl, 2002, p. 7). Consider again the case of a firm maximizing profits within a free competitive market. This firm maximizes profits with the market conditions *given* to him. The *alertness* of this firm and his use of market information does not change the market structure, or does so only marginally. But a central bank is a Big Player in the sense that their own behavior changes the market structure and incentives of economic agents. For a Big Player, market conditions are not just given to them, but once they execute a strategy, such conditions change triggering a different behavior on the part of economic agents. Choosing the optimal strategy requires being able to foresee the unintended and unforeseeable consequences that following a given strategy would trigger.[12] In other words, the central banker needs to be able to foresee what would be the optimal policy in a "state of nature" that does not exist and therefore there is no information to "calibrate" this alternative scenario. This problem can be illustrated in terms of game theory. Consider a game where the central bank is one player facing a number of possible strategies (monetary policies). In a typical game, the payoff of its strategy depends on its strategy, the other player's strategies and on the conditions of the game (market structure). But the Big Player effect means that every time the central bank choses a strategy, the rules of the game and the payoffs of the strategy change. As a player, the central bank does not only need to foresee the other player's strategies, it also needs to foresee what the new game will look like. This is why Hayek's knowledge problem in central banking requires policy makers to have an *alertness* skill that transcends reading the market as given, but also being able to *correctly* foresee a non-existent market condition that depends on what course of action the central bank does or does not take. The problem becomes even more challenging when there is more than one Big Player involved, as is the case of major central banks reacting differently to the Federal Reserve's monetary policy.

In turn, the Big Player effect also makes it harder for economic agents to predict and correctly read the market situation. It is not the same for a producer to predict a *pattern* of economic effects such as inflation than have to predict the behavior of a Big Player that implies being able to foretell the political motivations and psychology of policy makers. To predict a pattern of economic cause–effect and the behavior of a policy maker are two different types of problem. It is possible that an economic agent has an efficient *alertness* regarding the economy but an inefficient one with respect to the policy-maker behavior (or the other way around). This means that this producer would correctly predict the economic consequences of a monetary policy, but would wrongly predict which monetary policy is going to be executed. This can become a significant issue during a crisis when policy makers are trying to contain the downturn in different ways. Finally, another consequence of the effects of a Big Player such as a central bank, is that a change in policy can scramble the Type-B errors when the structure of the economy is affected.

Cantillon Effect

Following Cantillon's (1755, Chapter V) discussion, the Cantillon Effect refers to the effect produced on relative prices by a change in money supply. This effect depends on the injection point of the new money supply. Since resource allocation depends on relative prices, then change in money supply affects resource allocation. This effect occurs regardless of whether the money is a commodity or fiat. In turn, the Cantillon Effect leads to the signal extraction problem. It is too difficult for economic agents to know which prices (and to what extent) are having a nominal shock at any point in time. The intuition behind the Cantillon Effect is that the flow of new money affects prices sequentially as the new money flows through the market. Cantillon Effects occur either due to a change in money supply or to a change in money demand that would change the amount and pattern of spending. Cantillon is writing in the context of a commodity money such as gold, because of this the Cantillon Effect is usually framed in the context of a new inflow of gold into the economy. But a change in how a given stock of money flows through the economy would still be consistent with Cantillon's argument. A central bank that changes money supply will also produce a Cantillon Effect.

Assume the central bank decides to monetize a deficit for which it creates new money that is given *first* to the government in exchange for treasury bonds. In this case the government is in the privileged position of being able to spend the new money *before* prices have risen. Since the new money has not been spent yet, the first recipient of the new supply of money can spend it before they have lost any purchasing power. Whoever the recipients are of the increased government spending can spend their new income when prices have increased only slightly. This sequence continues until the new money supply reaches the last of all economic agents. Whoever is last in line is in the opposite situation to that of the government. The last recipient of the new money supply can spend his share of new money *after* prices have increased. This is why inflation redistributes wealth and is also why it is considered to be a non-legislated tax when the first recipient of the new supply of money is the government. The government, rather than taxing away monetary *units* from economic agents, seizes part of their *purchasing power*. Note that the effects of the above discussion do not change if the injection point (the first recipient of the change in money supply) is not the government. The issue remains that the demand for different goods and services will change at different points in time depending on how the new money supply flows through all economic agents. A different entry point of the new money supply produces a different pattern in the flow of money and therefore, relativly, will change differently.

Cantillon Effects usually refer to the case of changes in money supply. The argument can be extended to the case of a fixed money supply and a change in the pattern of spending. For instance, if we assume instead that the deficit is financed by issuing treasury bonds sold to the market rather than by expanding money supply, then money would be diverted from its usual flow in the economy toward the treasury's expenditures. In this particular case, because there is no increase in money supply, there is no increase in the price level. But the change in the flow of money affects different prices at different points of time and relative prices will change to reflect the new spending pattern. If spending changes because of a change in preferences, the relative prices would adjust to reflect the new consumer wants. Cantillon Effects, however, usually refer to changes in relative prices that do not reflect equilibrium conditions or changes in market fundamentals such as consumer preferences.

There is a difference to point out between Cantillon Effects under central banking and under free banking. In the former case, there is *one* source of changes in money supply and therefore the Cantillon Effect has a larger or stronger injection point in the economy. In the latter case, there are multiple injection points of money supply: each commercial bank that issues convertible banknotes. This makes the pattern of money flow in the economy more evenly distributed and less costly if relative prices are affected in the wrong way. But the case of free banking does not only have a larger amount of smaller injection points with respect to central banking, these injection points are also matched to the sources of the changes in money demand since those banks that will expand their money supply are the same ones that see their reserves increase due to increase in money demand of their depositors. These banks, in turn, are competing to fund the best investment options with new credit lines rather than having the primary dealers as the first recipients of an increase in money supply. For instance, a free bank may issue a credit to a wrong line of business. But this bank is competing with other free banks also trying to discover the correct new lines of investment. It is unlikely that under free banking relative prices will be distorted in a significant way.

It is important to note that the fact that central banks use the newly created money to buy financial assets from banks, leaving the size of their balance sheets unchanged, does not mean there are no Cantillon Effects either. Banks that engage in this open market operation have a preference of reserves over financial assets. The balance sheet of the banks may not change in size, but their composition does. If the new reserves are used to extend new loans, then the money flow sequence discussed above produces changes in relative prices nonetheless. Cantillon Effects are not just about what happens to the *first* recipient of a new supply of money, but about the *whole* effect the change in money supply produces on relative price.

It might be argued that in many cases Cantillon Effects are not large enough to become a significant economic disturbance. However, the Cantillon Effect can become significant if its reach is magnified by other factors such as market regulations. In the years prior to the 2008 crisis, new regulation and political pressure channeled the loose monetary policy of the Federal Reserve that took place after 2001 toward the real estate market, contributing to the housing bubble (see next chapter). For instance, to the extent that there was a loose monetary policy that fueled the housing bubble of the 2008 crisis, monetary policy can produce a Cantillon Effect with serious consequences to the rest of the economy.[13] In addition, as discussed in the last section of the previous chapter, an increase of money supply that is channeled through the financial market produces an increase in the supply of *credit* and therefore the price of credit, the interest rate, falls. As discount rates used by investors move downward, the present value of the cash-flow of different projects changes differently according to their *duration*. The relative change of present values (which are prices as well) is also a type of Cantillon Effect.

Cantillon Effects and money neutrality as an assumption

Since Cantillon Effects relate to resource allocation through changes in relative prices, it seems that this idea and the principle of money neutrality are at odds with each other. Money neutrality is understood as the condition that the level of output does not depend on the supply of money in the *long-run*. Since output is constrained by productivity and the endowment of factors of production, changes in the money supply have a nominal effect only. Still, it is acknowledged that in the *short-run* changes in money supply can have real effects, for instance through wage stickiness. In principle, Cantillon Effects and money neutrality could be consistent with each other in the following way. While Cantillon Effects describes the short-run effects on relative prices of a shock to money supply, money neutral-ity speaks about the final situation once the effect of the nominal shock goes away. In other words, a shock to money supply may change the *path* through which the economy approaches equilibrium, but it does not change the *equilibrium* point.

However, a difference remains between money neutrality and Cantillon Effects. The former is usually framed in the context of macroeconomic models, where aggre-gates are more important than relative prices. To the extent that relative prices take place in macroeconomic models, they are of an aggregate nature, such as the average nominal wage over a price index. The Cantillon Effect, however, is about changes to relative prices at the micro level. Let $w_i = \{w_1; \ldots; w_N\}$ represent each particular wage in the labor market and $p_j = \{p_1; \ldots; p_M\}$ the price of each particular consumer good in the economy where W and P represent the wage index and price index respectively. While macroeconomics is usually focused with what happens to $\left(\frac{W}{P}\right)$ when there is a monetary shock, the Cantillon Effect refers to the changes in the relative prices of all w_i and p_j.[14] This difference is important not only because Cantillon Effects have a dif-ferent scope than macro money neutrality, but because the same value of $\left(\frac{W}{P}\right)$ can be achieved with *different* sets of values for w_i and p_j. This is relevant because resource allocation depends on the relative prices at the micro level. At the macroeconomic level, the non-neutrality of money in the short-run can be expressed in the difference between ΔW and ΔP. But Cantillon Effects are about shocks of an unknown distribu-tion to each particular w_i and p_j; the macroeconomic setting minimizing the issue of the signal extraction problem that a change of money supply produces.

If this is the case, if resource allocation depends on relative prices at the micro-economic level, then the principle of money neutrality needs to say more than the level of output is independent of the price level, it also needs to sustain that *all* relative prices in equilibrium remain unchanged. This statement requires that the final (equilibrium) positions of the demand and supply of all goods (intermediate and final) would remain unchanged in the long-run in the presence of a nominal shock. For this to happen, a monetary shock and its short-run effects should have an effect neither on consumer preferences (demand) nor on the endowment of the factors of production (supply). But there is no reason to sustain that consumer preferences would not be affected by the short-run changes produced by a mon-etary shock. And there is also no reason why the endowment of the factors of production would not change due to the short-run Cantillon Effects. As long as factors of production have a certain degree of heterogeneity and irreversibility, once they are applied to a given production process, it is to be expected that the endowment of factors of production will change in composition. Some factors of production can become a waste if they are irrecoverable and were invested in an unprofitable line of business that went bankrupt after the monetary shock effect dissipated. The total endowment of factors of production could actually be reduced. In his Nobel Lecture, (Friedman, 1976) argues that it is possible for the Phillips Curve to have a positive slope. For instance, long periods of high inflation that result in loss of capital goods coupled with sticky wages (when wages move slower than prices of final goods) will produce a higher unemployment rate than if wages can adjust to their lower productivity levels (Ravier, 2010; 2013).

Money neutrality is more an assumption than a fact and, as such, it can be useful or misleading depending when and how it is applied. The use of the money neutrality assumption can help to isolate the long-run microeconomic effects of monetary shock. But it can be misleading if it is taken as a fact and monetary policy is designed assuming the micro effects of a change in monetary policy are only temporary. To put it differently, at the macroeconomic level, money neutrality means that the economy eventually goes back to the production possibilities frontier (PPF). But for this to have a specific and useful meaning, the economy needs to return always to the *same* point on the PPF. However, as long as a change in monetary policy changes either preferences or the endowment of factors of production, the economy will converge to a *different* point on the PPF after a monetary shock even if we assume that the PPF size is independent of nominal shocks.

Reducing the knowledge problem gap

The above discussion suggests that central banking faces problems that are beyond choosing, designing, and implementing the right monetary policy. Central bankers also face a knowledge problem. Policy making is more than just a technical problem of calibrating variables by the right amount at the right time. In the words of White (2010), monetary authorities are not constrained by the *rule of law*, which becomes particularly important during difficult times. And if there is no *rule of law*, then there is the *rule of the authority* or, in this case, the *rule of the expert*. This means discretion, and therefore uncertainty such as bailout policies or new market regulations. It also means that central bankers not only choose how to run monetary policy, they may also be able to change the scope of the monetary institutions. Hummel (2011), for instance, argues that under Ben Bernanke the Federal Reserve started to behave as a central planner under the umbrella of monetary policy.

To reduce the gap between the information and knowledge that a central bank needs to efficiently mimic monetary equilibrium under free banking and the information and knowledge that is actually available, an institutional reform that would move monetary institutions closer to a free-banking regime is necessary. These reforms do not consist of changing *how* to do monetary policy, but a change in the constitutional or meta-rules of monetary policy. The problem is how to give room to market forces that produce the information and incentives for the market to achieve equilibrium on its own without so much reliance on the central bank. The more powerful a central bank is, and the more control it has over the economy, the more challenging its job and the more costly its mistakes become. Some of the potential reforms, such as an NGDP future's market and Hayek's currency competition, are discussed in the last chapter. But before turning to these and other monetary reforms, it is time now to spend some time discussing the 2008 crisis.

Notes

1 Surely, central banks avoid making losses. But that does not mean that profit maximization is what drives monetary policy.
2 The situation of accidental discoveries of gold was discussed in Chapter 1. Also see White (1999, Chapter 2).
3 For instance, the Federal Reserve operates with around twenty primary dealers.
4 Other primary dealers that followed a risky investment strategy were Citigroup Global Markets Inc., Merrill Lynch Government Securities Inc., and Bear, Stearns, & Co. Inc.
5 Hogan and Manish (2016) discuss the knowledge problem applied to financial regulation.
6 Boettke and O'Donnell (2013) argue that Hayek has been misunderstood and misapplied in neoclassical economics. Also see N. Cachanosky and Padilla (2017). For a discussion on Hayek's arguments against the socialist calculation debate see Caldwell (1997), Coyne, Leeson, and Boettke (2005), Kirzner (1988), Lavoie (1981), and Yeager (1994).
7 Let us assume that market demand depends on consumer preferences and supply depends on technology and the endowment of factors of production. On the demand side, preferences are not observable. On the supply side, what constitutes technology and a factor of production is also not objectively given, it also depends on the subjective interpretation of these assets. Without a market process to channel consumer preferences, goods cannot be given the meaning of a factor of production. For instance, whether the object we call a "hammer" is a factor of production or a consumption good (i.e. hanging on a wall for decoration) depends on consumer preferences, not on objective physical qualities of the hammer.
8 For an illustration of the implications of the difference between information and knowledge see the exchange between Becker (1962; 1963) and Kirzner (1962; 1963).
9 For a financial framework of Kirzner's *alertness* see the discussion in N. Cachanosky (2017).
10 See the discussion and references included in Chapter 1.
11 Consider the discussion about the relative performance of the Federal Reserve of the United States with far from perfect and competitive monetary regimes by Selgin, Lastrapes, and White (2012) and the subsequent discussion articles that follow in the same journal edition. Also see Hogan (2015).
12 This analysis of course resembles the Lucas Critique.
13 Anderson (1949) and J. C. Cachanosky (1989) argue that the financial crisis that triggered the Great Depression had a similar format to the 2008 housing bubble. In the years prior to the stock exchange crash the Federal Reserve was channeling new money supply through financial brokers that invested the funds in the stock exchange. The two largest crises in the United States can be interpreted as the result of a magnified Cantillon Effect.
14 Cantillon Effects, of course, have a larger reach than just w_i and p_j, as it also includes the price of intermediate goods, the interest rate, and any other relevant price in the economy.

References

Anderson, B. M. (1949). *Economics and the Public Welfare* (1980 ed.). Indianapolis: Liberty Fund.
Becker, G. S. (1962). Irrational Behavior and Economic Theory. *Journal of Political Economy*, 70.(1): 1–13.

Becker, G. S. (1963). Rational Action and Economic Theory: A Reply to I. Kirzner. *Journal of Political Economy*, 71.(1): 82–83.

Boettke, P. J., and O'Donnell, K. W. (2013). The Failed Appropriation of F. A. Hayek by Formalist Economics. *Critical Review*, 25.(3–4): 305–341.

Cachanosky, J. C. (1989). La Crisis del Treinta. *Libertas*, 10.(Mayo).

Cachanosky, N. (2017). Austrian Economics, Market Process, and the EVA® Framework. *Journal of Business Valuation and Economic Loss Analysis*, 12.(s1).

Cachanosky, N., and Padilla, A. (2017). Economic and Philosophical Implications of Hayek's Knowledge Problem. *Libertas: Segunda Epoca*, 2.(1): 67–79.

Caldwell, B. J. (1997). Hayek and Socialism. *Journal of Economic Literature*, 35.(4): 1856–1890.

Cantillon, R. (1755 [1959]). *Essai Sur La Nature du Commerce en Général*. London: Frank Cass and Company Ltd.

Coyne, C. J., Leeson, P. T., and Boettke, P. J. (2005). Hayek vs. the Neoclassicists: Lessons from the Socialist Calculation Debate. In N. Barry (Ed.), *Elgar Companion to Hayekian Economics*. Cheltenham: Edward Elgar Publishing.

Friedman, M. (1976). Inflation and Unemployment. *Nobel Memorial Lecture*.

Hayek, F. A. (1948). *Individualism and Economic Order*. Chicago: University of Chicago Press.

Hogan, T. L. (2015). Has the Fed Improved U.S. Economic Performance? *Journal of Macroeconomics*, 43.(March): 257–266.

Hogan, T. L., and Manish, G. P. (2016). Banking Regulation and Knowledge Problems. *Advances in Austrian Economoics*, 20: 213–234.

Hummel, J. R. (2011). Ben Bernanke versus Milton Friedman. The Federal Reserve's Emergence as the U.S. Economy's Central Planner. *The Independent Review*, 15.(4): 485–518.

Kirzner, I. M. (1962). Rational Action and Economic Theory. *The Journal of Political Economy*, 70.(4): 380–385.

Kirzner, I. M. (1963). Rational Action and Economic Theory: Rejoinder. *The Journal of Political Economy*, 71.(1): 84–85.

Kirzner, I. M. (1973). *Competition and Entrepreneurship*. Chicago: University of Chicago Press.

Kirzner, I. M. (1988). The Economic Calculation Debate: Lessons for Austrians. *The Review of Austrian Economics*, 2: 1–18.

Kirzner, I. M. (1992). *The Meaning of Market Process*. New York: Routledge.

Koppl, R. G. (2002). *Big Players and the Economic Theory of Expectations*. New York: Palgrave Macmillan.

Lavoie, D. C. (1981). A Critique of the Standard Account of the Socialist Calculation Debate. *The Journal of Libertarian Studies*, 5.(1): 41–87.

Ravier, A. O. (2010). *En Busca del Pleno Empleo. Estudios de Macroeconomía Austríaca y Economía Comparada*. Madrid, Spain: Unión Editorial.

Ravier, A. O. (2013). Dynamic Monetary Theory and the Phillips Curve with a Positive Slope. *Quarterly Journal of Austrian Economics*, 16.(2): 165–186.

Salter, A. W. (2013). Not All NGDP Is Created Equal: A Critique of Market Monetarism. *Journal of Private Enterprise*, XXIX.(1): 41–52.

Salter, A. W., and Smith, D. J. (2017). What You Don't Know Can Hurt You: Knowledge Problems in Monetary Policy. *Contemporary Economic Policy*, 35.(3): 505–517.

Selgin, G. A. (1988). *The Theory of Free Banking*. Lanham: CATO Institute and Rowman & Littlefield.

Selgin, G. A., Lastrapes, W. D., and White, L. H. (2012). Has the Fed Been a Failure? *Journal of Macroeconomics*, 34.(3): 569–596.

White, L. H. (1999). *The Theory of Monetary Institutions*. Oxford: Basil Blackwell.

White, L. H. (2010). The Rule of Law or the Rule of Central Bankers? *Cato Journal*, 30.(3): 451–463.

Yeager, L. B. (1994). Mises and Hayek on Calculation and Knowledge. *The Review of Austrian Economics*, 7.(2): 93–109.

Zanotti, G. J. (2011). *Conocimiento versus Información*. Madrid: Union Editorial.

6   The 2008 financial crisis

Introduction

The 2008 crisis is one of the largest and more complex events in the U.S. economic history. No less for the fact that its center is located in the financial markets, a highly specialized activity without much presence in standard macroeconomic models such as dynamic stochastic general equilibrium models. Still, the unfolding of the crisis is consistent with much of the discussion presented so far in this book. Surely, a nominal income targeting framework does not suffice to explain the crisis completely, but it is a necessary framework to understand the economic effects at a broader scale.

The renewed interest in nominal income targeting is not accidental, it coincides with the fact that an event as significant as the 2008 was not, and cannot, be predicted or explained with conventional macroeconomic models (Blanchard, 2014; 2016; Blanchard, Dell'Ariccia, and Mauro, 2010; Caballero, 2010; Keen, 2018; Romer, forthcoming; Stiglitz, 2011). In addition, the 2008 crisis fits better the scenario of nominal shock than it does one with a real shock. There are two distinctive characteristics regarding the housing crisis of the 2008 crisis, how it was built in the first place and why did it happen in the housing market in particular. In turn, the analysis of the crisis can be separated in two different questions: why was it so severe and why did it last so long?

To answer the above questions, the chapter is structured in the following way. The next section discusses the building of the crisis. The third section discusses the monetary policy after the crisis. The last section discusses alternative explanations of the crisis such as the savings glut hypothesis.

The building of the crisis

It is hard to sustain that the sharp fall in aggregate demand in the 2008 crisis was driven by an irrational behavior in a market operated by highly trained specialists using complex and new financial instruments. If irrationality cannot be explained, then it does not amount to much of an explanation. This line of arguing would also require that somehow the irrational behavior was not only significant enough, but also that this irrational behavior occurred simultaneously across a number

Table 6.1 Stance of monetary policy before the 2008 crisis with respect to selected benchmarks

Benchmark	Expansionary monetary policy?	Period
Taylor rule	Yes	2002–2006
Deviation from the natural rate of interest (Laubach and Williams)	Yes	2001–2006
Deviation from the natural rate of interest (Selgin, Beckworth, Bahadir)	Yes	2001–2006
NGDP trend deviation	Yes	2005–2008
GO/GDP	Yes	2007–2008
Prices of factors of production growing faster than price of final goods	Yes	2001–2007
Young's roundaboutness	Yes	2002–2005

of economic agents large enough produce and burst the housing bubble. On the contrary, empirical evidence suggests that the building of the housing bubble originated in a monetary policy deviation by major central banks rather than just on irrational exuberance.

Especially after the 2001 dotcom crisis, the U.S. Federal Reserve moved to a loose monetary policy with the intention of avoiding a downturn of the economy. This change in policy was sharp enough to move the federal funds rate to historically low levels. Different benchmarks discussed in previous chapters suggest that monetary policy was too expansionary (Table 6.1). There is no need to show the graphics and numbers again, a summary of their results suffices. The important message of Table 6.1 is that all of them point to an expansionary monetary policy in the years prior to the crisis.

Bernanke (2013, pp. 51–53) denies that the low interest rates in the years prior to the crisis were a major fuel to the housing bubble, but he does also admit that monetary policy was easier "to help the economy recover from the 2001 recession" (p. 101). Interestingly, Ahrend, Cournède, and Price (2008) find that those countries with the largest deviations from their Taylor rule prescription were the ones showing the largest housing bubbles as well. In financial terms, housing is a good with a long-term service of consumption (or cash-flow through rent payment), and as such its price (present value) is more sensitive than other consumer goods to movements in discount rates.

The issue with arguments such as Bernanke's is that they do not connect the doing of monetary policy with the institutional framework (and therefore economic agents' incentives) in which policy is taking place. Since money is not injected into the economy through a helicopter, the injection point *and* the institutional framework become a required piece of information to understand why the cluster of errors (or a bubble) is located in any particular market. Given a particular injection point of liquidity, the institutions and regulation in place can channel the excess of liquidity through particular sectors of the economy. Even then a housing bubble should not be a surprising event. Due to their long-term service (in providing shelter), the housing market is particularly sensitive to changes in the discount rates. Bernanke (2013) mentions more than once that one of the objectives of a low interest rate policy is to boost the housing market. It should be expected, then, that record low nominal federal funds rates (and negative real rates for around two and a half years) would have a significant effect in the housing market. The housing bubble did not occur within an unregulated economy, but within an institutional framework that incentivized the housing market in particular.[1] In fact, a full understanding of how the easy monetary policy of the early 2000s ended in the housing market crisis requires going back a number of years when policy and regulations started to bend toward favoring house ownership.

The homeownership incentive in the Tax Reform Act of 1986 is probably the most well-known policy in the United States. However, government involvement with the housing market in the United States is not new. The Federal Housing Administration (FHA) was founded in 1934 with the objective to increase the level of home ownership during the Great Depression. The two main tools to achieve this objective were the control of mortgage rates and the terms of mortgage application such as down payment requirements. The FHA required a 20% down payment by the applicant to qualify for a backed mortgage. Four years later, in 1938 as part of Roosevelt's New Deal, Fannie Mae was founded with the mission to guarantee and take mortgage loans off the books of the Veteran's Association and the FHA (this was extended to conventional mortgages as well in the late 1960s). Freddie Mac joined this financial policy in 1970 by acquiring mortgages from the thrift, savings and loan industry. Freddie Mac was owned by the industry until 1989.

The participation of Fannie Mae and Freddie Mac, two government-sponsored enterprises (GSE), produced two financial problems that came to surface during the crisis. The first one was to concentrate, rather than diversify, mortgage risk in these two entities. The second one was that the GSEs worked under the *implicit* assumption that they had a government guarantee in case of financial failure. Because this bailout promise was implicit, rather than formally quantified and defined, it did not show up in the stock of government debt. This debt became a surprise of uncertain value during the 2008 crisis. Government debt was understated by an unknown amount. In short, GSEs played the role of an indirect and implicit (off the books) government bailout promise to mortgage lenders incentivizing an easy mortgage policy that increased the risk exposure to the housing market.

But these GSEs were hardly the only entities building incentives to issue mortgages carrying excessive risk. The Community Reinvestment Act (CRA), first enacted in 1977, also played an important role. For the first twelve years it was only required for commercial banks to inform the government of the loans extended to the same neighborhoods from where deposits were coming from. But two steps were taken that transformed the CRA into a driver of bank lending policies. First, in 1989 Congress made the CRA ratings public information. Second, in

1995 regulators were allowed to penalize banks with low CRA ratings by denying mergers or opening of new branches. In addition, a complaint from a neighborhood organization could underscore a bank's CRA rating. This provided neighborhood associations a powerful negotiation tool to channel credit toward their own neighborhoods. With these new powers, groups like the Association of Community Organizations for Reform Now (ACORN) started to pressure banks to issue loans in exchange for not filing a complaint. The unintended and unexpected result was for banks to partner with neighborhood associations and issue mortgages to otherwise unqualified recipients. Banks would also "buy" a higher CRA rating by acquiring CRA mortgage-backed securities, which were a financial portfolio with a high proportion of high-risk mortgages that were securitized by Freddie Mac.

In 1993 the Department of Housing and Urban Development (HUD) joined the political pressure to issue mortgage loans by initiating legal actions against mortgage issuers and GSEs that would deny mortgage loans in a higher proportion to minorities than to white applicants. Facing the threat of legal action and its associated costs, banks started to loosen the qualifications required to apply for a mortgage such as income and down payment. To fulfill this requirement, Fannie Mae and Freddie Mac had to increase their borrowing, which was done at a low interest rate due to the implicit bailout commitment by the Treasury. In 2000, it was announced that HUD will require that Fannie Mae allocate 50% of its business to low- and moderate-income families and spend up to $500 billion in CRA business by 2010.

The institutional framework has traditionally leaned toward favoring the demand side of the housing market. But this framework was not constant. At different points in time further amendments favoring home ownership were enacted that had significant impact on the housing market. In particular, the litigation attitude of HUD and the 1995 CRA reform. The effect of these institutional reforms biased the credit expansion toward the housing market. And, as an unintended consequence, the risk exposure of the mortgage market increased as more mortgages were granted from less to more risky recipients. Between 2001 and 2006, the share of new subprime mortgages issued increased from 10% to 34%. In addition, the share of subprime applicants not supplying a 20% down payment also increased. For the same period, the share of subprime mortgages in the mortgage market increased from 7.6% to 23.5%.

There were other unintended consequences of the housing policy that increased risk exposure in the financial market. The Federal Reserve's downward movement of the federal funds rate also moved the rate of the adjustable-rate mortgages (ARM) downward. In relative terms, ARMs became cheaper than fixed-rate mortgages. Because of this, a higher share of mortgage applications were issued as ARM. Also, holders of fixed mortgages swapped them for ARM. Because ARMs are riskier than fixed-rate mortgages, the overall risk of the mortgage market increased further.

Figure 6.1 shows the average monthly rate for fixed and adjustable mortgage rates between 1990 and 2015. In the second half of the 1990s both rates keep a relative constant difference, but starting in 2001 the ARM rate decreases at a faster

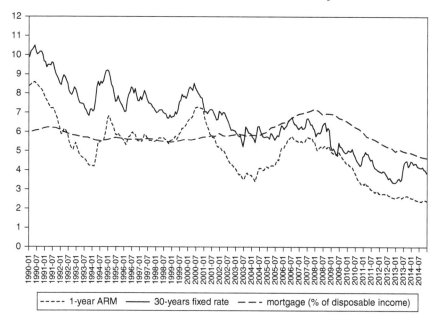

Figure 6.1 Monthly fixed and adjustable mortgage rates, United States, 1990–2015.
Source: Freddie Mac and Board of Governors of the Federal Reserve System.

rate than the fixed mortgage rates. Also, note that the ARM rates start to increase at the same time the Federal Reserve starts to increase the federal funds rate. This coincides with an increase in the mortgage debt service payments as percentage of disposable income. Even though this increase does not seem to be significant, according to the Federal Reserve Board of Governors, "this approximation is useful to the extent that, by using the same method and data series over time, it generates a time series that captures the important *changes* in the household debt service burden" (emphasis in original).[2] The *change* in the series starting in 2004 is significant. It took two years for this change to materialize in a higher level of delinquency at all commercial banks, going from 1.61% in the first quarter of 2006 to a peak of 11.53% in 2010.

The time series of house prices is also informative (Figure 6.2). A particular point of interest is that in the United States house prices start to increase before 2001. At first sight this would contradict the thesis that the housing bubble was fueled by the Federal Reserve's monetary policy. But, a closer look shows that this is still consistent with the easy monetary policy that took place after 2001 as the main driver of the boom. In short, two different effects following each other make the series look *as if* the boom started in the late 1990s. There are a few reasons that can explain the increase in prices prior to 2001. One of them is an inflow of funds invested in the real-estate market as a result of the financial crisis in Asia, Russia, and different parts of the world. Another reason is a wealth effect from the dotcom bubble that has not burst yet. A third reason is that the increase in house

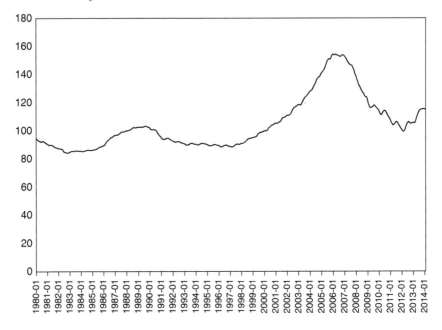

Figure 6.2 S&P/Case–Shiller U.S. National Home Price Index ©.
Source: S&P Dow Jones Indices LLC.

prices started shortly after the CRA reform and that the HUD initiated its litigation attitude against banks. In real terms, house prices were at the same level in 2001 as at the peak of 1989. It is after the low interest rate policy that started in 2001 when house prices steadily increased beyond previous peaks. Even if house prices started to increase in the late 1990s, the reasons that explain the rise in house prices are not enough to explain the size of the housing bubble.

Why the crisis was so deep

Explaining why there was a housing bubble is a different issue from explaining why the economic crisis was so deep. And this is probably the main reason why NGDP Targeting gained momentum after the 2008 crisis. The reasoning is well captured by Sumner (2012, p. 14), who asserts that in "the late 1990s and early 2000s a severe decline in NGDP caused a financial crisis in Argentina. Then, in 2008–2009, falling NGDP in the United States and Europe caused a relatively modest financial crisis to become much larger."

This reasoning requires a qualification. Taking in its literal meaning, the first reference implies that the Argentine crisis of 2001 was caused *by* a decline in NGDP, *not* by its accumulated fiscal deficit, default of sovereign debt, confiscation of bank deposits, etc. A fall in NGDP is a fall in aggregate demand, which is in itself the definition of a crisis. A severe decline in NGDP cannot be the explanation of a severe decline in NGDP. It is the fall in NGDP that needs to be explained,

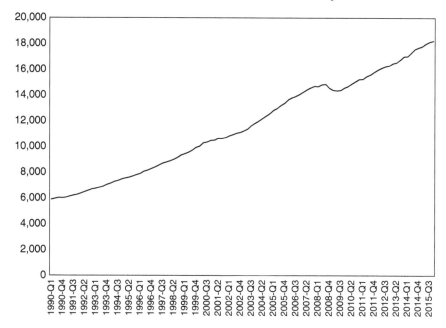

Figure 6.3 Quarterly NGDP, United States, 1990–2015.

Source: U.S. Bureau of Economic Analysis, Gross Domestic Product [GDP].

for instance due to a monetary policy mistake. The reference to the NGDP fall in the United States and Europe is more accurate, in the sense it clarifies that what a fall in NGDP causes is to transform a relatively modest financial crisis into a much larger crisis. This Market Monetarism explanation has some similarity to the monetarist explanation of the Great Depression. The two largest economic crises in the United States are explained by a mistake on the part of the Federal Reserve. Figure 6.3 shows that in 2008, NGDP falls and it does not return to its previous level, which is the main point of the Market Monetarism NGDP Targeting.

The NGDP series offers a few lessons. First, as mentioned in Chapter 4, the fact that economic variables look good in the years prior to the crisis does not mean that the economy is actually in good shape. The fact that a good economic situation yields good economic indicators, does not mean we can infer from good economic indicators that the economy is in good shape (*post hoc ergo propter hoc* fallacy). The fact that in the years prior to the crisis the main economic indicators, such as inflation, unemployment, and GDP volatility, showed no signs of economic problems does not mean that imbalances were not taking place. As discussed in Chapter 4, a closer look shows signs that the 4% growth rate of NGDP might have been the result of a loose monetary policy.

Second, it shows that monetary policy was tight, rather than loose, during the crisis. The fall in NGDP means that money supply was not loose enough to compensate for the fall in money velocity. For a few reasons, this does not necessarily contradict the low interest rate observed after 2008. A low interest rate can be explained by an increase in supply (a loose monetary policy), but also by a fall in demand. Two reasons can explain a low demand for credit. One is that, because investment is irreversible, the increase in *regime uncertainty* decreased the demand for credit to start new business projects (Dixit and Pyndick, 1994; Higgs, 2009.) The other is that the significant increase in reserves by banks at the Federal Reserve reduced the demand of credit in the federal funds market.

Third, if the problem of the crisis were just the fall in NGDP, it would be expected that once market expectations adapt to the new level of NGDP the crisis would revert as spending increases. But the sluggish recovery from the crisis suggested that there was something other driving the crisis than the fall of NGDP from its level. Given that the nominal effects were captured in NGDP movements, the other factors present in the crisis were to be found in the real sector. Apart from clear real shocks, the likely reason is a cluster misallocation of heterogeneous resources (physical capital and labor as well) during the *too low for too long* interest rate policy of the Federal Reserve (the Cantillon Effect discussed in Chapter 5).

The severity of the crisis can be explained by coupling the financial costs of mortgage delinquency with the Federal Reserve failure to stabilize NGDP. While prior to the Great Depression, a loose monetary policy channeled new credit to the stock exchange through financial brokers, prior to the 2008 crisis the new credit was channeled through mortgage issuers to the housing market. The expansionary policy that started in 2001 also incentivized the development of complex financial instruments that are hard to accurately price and whose risk is hard to assess. It is more likely that an excess of liquidity due to the easy monetary policy starting in 2001 contributed to the development of complex financial instruments and the housing bubble, rather than complex financial instruments being enough to fuel the housing bubble. The development of these complex financial institutions is another *unintended consequence* of the monetary policy that started in 2001 and its interaction with the housing market.

After the crisis

Monetary policy

The 2008 financial crisis is characterized by a sequence of unexpected costs taking place in the financial market. Unexpectedly, financial assets that were supposed to be safe lost their market value, seriously affecting the balance sheet of large institutions. The specific location of these costs remained hidden behind securitized assets that were supposed to be low risk. The securitization of mortgages contributed to diversify risk globally. But it also made it difficult for monetary authorities to know where financial trouble could be located as some financial institutions were either not required to provide the information to their central banks or were located outside the scope of the Federal Reserve authority (i.e. foreign banks). Before the end of 2008, the nominal federal funds rate was below 1%. Given this zero-lower-bound *conventional* limitation, the Federal Reserve and other major central banks started to execute *unconventional* monetary policy such as quantitative (and qualitative) easing and paying interest on reserves.[3]

A first major financial event was the failure of Bear Stearns in March 2008, which was bought by JP Morgan Chase with assistance from the Federal Reserve. The assistance of $30 billion was channeled to Bear Stearns through a limited liability company, Maiden Lane I, created for such specific purpose.[4] The reason the Federal Reserve assisted in this purchase was that JP Morgan was not confident of the investment grade status of Bear Stearn's mortgage-backed securities (MBS). Maiden Lane I, was a way for the Federal Reserve to execute an indirect bailout. This bailout was to the benefit of an institution with a questionable solvency situation, but that was considered *too big to fail*. The bailout's focus on the *too big to fail* (or *too interconnected to fail*) challenges Bernanke's (2013) assertion that the Federal Reserve closely followed Bagehot's rule (Hogan, Le, and Salter, 2015).

The financial situation turned worse when it became patent that Fannie Mae and Freddie Mac were insolvent. The government decided to put them into "conservatorship" (a limited bankruptcy situation) and the Treasury, with authorization from the government, backed the GSEs MBS. By doing this, the implicit insurance provided by the Treasury to GSEs securities was recognized. The rationale for the government to save the GSEs was, again, primarily that these institutions were *too big to fail*, not their solvency. If the Federal Reserve had followed Bagehot's rule as their main principle, the GSEs should have been allowed to fail and be financially liquidated.

Only a few days after the GSEs conservatorship, Merrill Lynch (a broker dealer) was bought by Bank of America. Lehman Brothers (another broker dealer) filed for bankruptcy on the same day. Lehman Brother's failure became a major turning point in the development of the crisis. According to Bernanke (2013, p. 94), the Federal Reserve did not bailout Lehman Brothers because it was an insolvent institution, and Bagehot's rule advises against bailing out insolvent entities. This contrasts with the Federal Reserve's assistance to JP Morgan to buy Bear Stearns who were not clearly solvent.[5] Even though the MBS being bought by JP Morgan Chase were investment grade, their market value was far from certain. The indirect bailouts of the Federal Reserve had the effect of increasing the *moral hazard* behavior of financial institutions. In other words, the Federal Reserve's behavior locked the expectation of Lehman Brothers and other financial institutions on the availability of bailout funds. The next day, American Insurance Group (AIG) became the target of financial pressure. AIG, which is also a thrift institution, had been selling insurance to the credit market, and the failure of Lehman Brothers brought doubts about its solvency.[6] AIG received financial assistance from the Federal Reserve through Maiden Lane II, and III. This series of events was followed by failure of large financial institutions such as Washington Mutual and Wachovia.

The reason why some institutions received financial assistance and others did not is whether or not such institutions were considered *too big to fail*. A bank is *too big to fail* if its size and interconnectedness is such that its failure can trigger a financial crisis similar to a domino effect. Rather than providing liquidity in general, the Federal Reserve, and the Treasury as well, were more inclined to provide focused assistance to those institutions in financial need that could endanger the whole financial market and target the specific financial assets in trouble. One of the programs built on this principle was the Trouble Asset Relief Program (TARP) run by the Treasury between October 2008 and December 2014. Under TARP, the Treasury would spend up to $475 billion dollars in buying specifically "toxic" financial assets from financial institutions.[7] The market for these financial assets was dry and TARP was aimed not only at improving the financial health of the recipients, but it also expected it would trigger an improvement in the value and trade opportunities for these assets. This healing of the financial institutions' balance sheets would also help the institutions to gain confidence in returning to the inter-banking credit market.

The Federal Reserve did its part with three series of quantitative easing (QEI, QEII, and QEIII). The conventional way of conducting monetary policy would be for the Federal Reserve to buy and sell in open market operations Treasury bonds. But, under QE, the Federal Reserve would also buy MBS. The first round of QEI starts in late 2008 with a budget of $600 billion to acquire MBS. The second round, QEII, started in late 2010 with a similar budget to QEI. QEIII differs from its predecessors in an important way: QEIII allocates a $40 billion budget per month without a maturity date and without a pre-stipulated budget limitation. Before the end of the year the monthly budget was more than doubled to $85 billion. It seems that by the third round of quantitative easing the remaining amount of financial assistance required was unknown. QEIII ended in late 2014.

Along with this unconventional policy framework, and with the objective of efficiently stimulating the economy, the Federal Reserve carried on "Operation Twist." Under this policy, the Federal Reserve sold short-term bonds and bought long-term bonds. This type of market operation twists, or changes, the slope of the yield curve by pushing down long-term interest rates and pushing up short-term interest rates. The rationale for twisting the yield curve this way is that investment decisions depend more on long-term interest rates than on short-term interest rates. Operation Twist was intended to have a larger impact on the economic recovery than short-term interest rates (which were also already on the lower-zero bound). The Federal Reserve's Operation Twist deviated from the conventional approach in the sense that it was intended to lower long-term interest rates *without* increasing short-term interest rates. The other reason to target long-term interest rates is that the Federal Reserve started to lose control of the short-term rates given the significant increase of reserves held by the banks as part of the different bailout programs.

The solid expansionary policy channeled through different unconventional programs begs the question of why NGDP failed to return to its level after it fell in 2008. This persistent fall in NGDP's trend was another unintended effect of a new tool of monetary policy. In this case, the payment of interest on total (required and excess) reserves that banks hold as deposits at the Federal Reserve played a significant role. Before being able to pay interest on reserves, the Federal Reserve extended loans through the discount window and sterilized such expansion by selling Treasury bonds. With this policy, the Federal Reserve eventually started to run out of Treasury bonds to sell, it was not possible to take out of circulation the excess of reserves through conventional channels anymore. The payment of interest on reserves started in late 2008. This policy had two objectives. One was to put a floor to the federal funds rate. If banks can receive risk-free interest by merely parking reserves at the Federal Reserve, then banks would not lend to each other at lower rates than the one they can receive free of risk from the Federal Reserve. This way the Federal Reserve would be able, in theory, to increase liquidity and increase the federal funds rate at the same time. The other objective was to reduce the amount of lending from banks to the rest of the economy to avoid inflation going above the Federal Reserve's target. By trying to avoid inflation, the Federal Reserve paid banks to not extend loans during the financial crisis. This design would allow the Federal Reserve to increase the liquidity of the financial institutions without adding pressure to inflation.

Intuitively, in terms of the quantity theory of money this policy would increase M and reduce V at the same time. The payment of interest on reserves would increase the demand of reserves by the banks and this would make money velocity fall. Money velocity of M2 fell from 1.94 in the first quarter of 2008 to 1.71 in the second quarter of 2009 (a 12% fall). The sharp fall in late 2008 coincides with the beginning of payments of interests on reserves (Figure 6.4). Other than a small

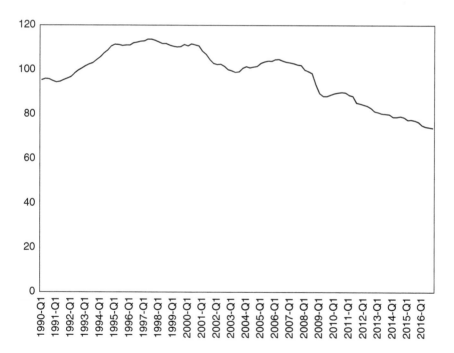

Figure 6.4 Velocity of M2, United States, 1990–2016 (2008 − Q1 = 100).

Source: U.S. Federal Reserve Bank of St. Louis.

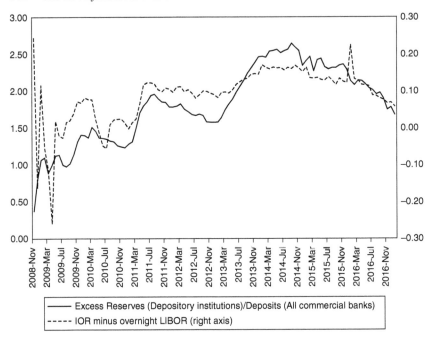

Figure 6.5 Excess reserves over total deposits and IOR-LIBOR spread, United States, 2008–2016.

Sources: Federal Reserve Bank of St. Louis, Board of Governors of the Federal Reserve System, and ICE Benchmark Administration Limited (IBA).

increase in 2010, M2 velocity kept falling to 1.44 in the fourth quarter of 2016. Since the first quarter of 2008 money velocity has fallen 25%. Figure 6.4 also shows that in 2003 money velocity starts to increase. M2, however, continued to increase, which also suggests a likely deviation from nominal income targeting in the years prior to the subprime crisis.

It can be argued that since the interest on reserves (IOR) is low, its impact on reserve hoarding would be insignificant. But the sharp increase in reserves says otherwise. As low as interest on reserves may seem, what matters is its relative value with respect to the bank's cost of opportunity. The higher the IOR, the more liquidity will remain at the Federal Reserve rather than being extended as loans to the market. The marginal dollar held as reserve at the Fed receives a risk-free interest. The alternative is the interest rate *margin* that it can receive if it is extended as a new loan. Note that while IOR is constant (horizontal) regardless of the amount deposited at the Federal Reserve, the demand of credit is downward sloping. Once the interest rate *margin* is equal to the interest on reserves, all extra dollars will be parked at the Federal Reserve. As Selgin (2017) points out, the ratio of reserves to total deposits follows the spread between IOR and the overnight LIBOR (London Inter-Bank Offered Rate) (Figure 6.5). To the extent that the Federal Reserve took into consideration that the IOR would go against increasing credit during the crisis, the sensitivity of banks to hold reserves in the presence of IOR was underestimated.

Moving toward monetary central planning

Hummel (2011) points to another important issue surrounding the Federal Reserve policy during the 2008 crisis, which is its movement toward a monetary central planning regime. To understand this, it is important to distinguish the monetary views of Alan Greenspan and Ben Bernanke. Changes in money supply and interest rates affect the whole economy; therefore it is hard for central banks to target specific sectors of the economy in isolation from the rest of the economy. However, to be specific regarding which assets to buy from the financial institutions and which banks to financially assist imply a different approach to conventional monetary policy. Hummel (2011) contrasts Bernanke's management of the crisis to Friedman and Schwartz.

For Friedman and Schwartz, because of sticky prices and wages, the focus during a crisis should be on nominal income. If there is a fall in nominal income, when prices cannot adjust fast enough, output will fall. Friedman's and Keynes's analysis share a common analytical framework but differ on *why* nominal income fell in the Great Depression. For Friedman, there is a fall in money supply due to a monetary policy mistake; for Keynes there is an increase in money demand because of the presence of animal spirits. For Bernanke (1983) the main problem is the collapse of the credit flow through the failure of financial intermediaries. In Bernanke's analysis this is interpreted as a shock to money velocity, since the bankruptcy of banks increases money demand by economic agents (Bernanke, 1988, pp. 8–10; Bernanke and Gertler, 1995).

As Hummel (2011, p. 487) argues, both views can be complements. However, different policy prescriptions are derived from each one of them. If the *main* problem is a fall in money supply, then an increase in liquidity is the main solution. But if the *main* problem is the fall of intermediaries, then the survival of important intermediaries is the *main* solution, especially those that would be too big to fail. Goodhart (1987) extends Bernanke's argument and holds that a movement of funds from one bank to another can have negative effects due to the transaction costs of allocating credit (knowing the customer, the particulars of each market, etc.). Liquidity might be restored, but the crisis would not be avoided if key intermediaries are out of the market and the flow of credit is nonetheless interrupted. Bernanke's view requires directing credit allocation to a specific institution and specific assets. And this requires a new *unconventional* approach to monetary policy. This view also requires a way to define which financial institutions are *too important to fail*. Not having a clear delimitation of institutions that should not be allowed to fail regardless of their solvency status adds uncertainty to the market. If this is the case, then financial institutions would be more inclined to spend more resources in being politically connected (i.e. lobbying or hiring politically connected individuals) if they expect this resources to work as a *synthetic* insurance toward a riskier behavior. Blau (2017) finds that financial institutions that were more politically connected during the 2008 crisis were more likely to receive emergency assistance from the Federal Reserve.

One of the first reactions to the crisis in late 2007 was the Term Auction Facility (TAF). The Federal Reserve discount window would traditionally set a discount rate and issue loans to banks. Under TAF, the Federal Reserve sets the amount of credit and the discount rate is determined by the bank's auction. Bernanke (2015, p. 157) explains that there were two reasons to offer this modified discount window to the financial market. One reason is that by setting the amount of liquidity rather than the discount rate, banks using the TAF would not face the stigma of paying a penalty rate to have access to liquidity. The second reason is that due to the auction process, it would take a few days for the banks to receive the liquidity, and therefore banks would not face the stigma of being in urgent need of liquidity. But how the TAF tool was implemented shows that for the Federal Reserve, credit and monetary controlled allocation was more important than general liquidity. At the same time the Federal Reserve was providing liquidity to the market, it was also sterilizing its own policy by selling Treasury bonds. Neither base money nor M2 show significant increases with this program (M1 does show an increase). TAF, intended or not, produced a change in the composition of M2, but not on its level. The Federal Reserve was changing reserves owned by the banks for reserves that the banks owed to the Federal Reserve. If liquidity were the main

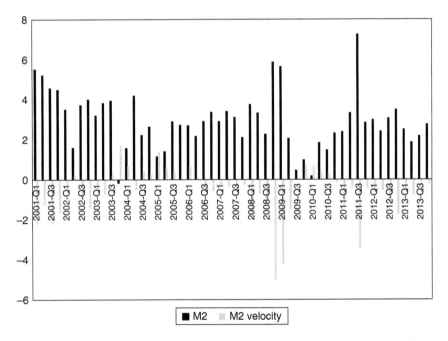

Figure 6.6 M2 and M2 velocity (seasonally adjusted) quarterly growth rates, United States, 2001–2013.

Sources: Board of Governors of the Federal Reserve System.

concern, then a traditional open market operation would suffice (where distribution of liquidity is to be determined by market participants) and sterilization by selling Treasury bonds would not have taken place, but TAF implied one step toward planning credit allocation. In terms of nominal income stability, M2 velocity was already falling by 2008, keeping monetary aggregate growth rates stable, rather than having them increase to offset the increase in money demand, implying a deviation from monetary equilibrium. As the sterilization of the liquidity injection from TAF was making the Federal Reserve run out of Treasury bonds, QE and paying interest on reserves became the new tools to manage credit allocation, in particular aiming toward long-term assets. Figure 6.6 shows that as money velocity starts to fall, M2 growth rate slows down between the first and third quarter of 2008. The impact on the start of the payment of interest on reserves is seen in the end of 2008 in Figure 6.6.

Following Hummel (2011), the monetary policy steps discussed above and the use of Maiden Lane subsidiaries to target not only specific assets, but also specific institutions considered *too big to fail* at the discretion of the Federal Reserve is a movement toward money or financial central planning. Deviations in the portfolios of financial institutions from what the Federal Reserve considered to be optimal can now be modified through monetary policy. The role of the central bank is not just to maintain monetary equilibrium anymore, but to dictate how liquidity should be allocated as well. If this vision of how monetary policy should be carried out is pushed to its limits, then financial institutions become *de facto* branches of the Federal Reserve.

The savings glut hypothesis

The excess savings, or savings glut view, argues that the housing bubble in particular, and the 2008 crisis in general, was not due to major central bank monetary policies, but to an excess of savings (Bernanke, 2005). The source of the excess of savings is the emerging economies which, due to lack of investment opportunities, and events such as a series of financial crises in the second half of the 1990s, migrated to developed economies. According to this view, an increase in global savings channeled to the U.S. is the source of the rising price of houses and low long-term interest rates.[8] Central banks had little role, if any, in the excess of liquidity that fed the housing bubble.

This view has not gone unchallenged (Borio and Disyatat, 2011; Bracke and Fidora, 2012; Hume and Sentance, 2009; Ryou, 2009). Hume and Sentance (2009) argue that current account imbalances, especially in the 2000s, do not provide a good match with this thesis. For instance, the reduction in U.S. long-term interest rates kept falling after a reversal in the current account. They sustain that the situation is likely to be the inverse: that current account imbalances were driven by the credit boom rather than the other way around.

Besides the current account behavior offering a weak support for the savings glut hypothesis, Borio and Disyatat (2011) also offer other critical points. First, according to the savings glut hypothesis, the inflow of funds to the U.S. should have resulted in an appreciation of the U.S. dollar. The U.S. dollar effective exchange rate, however, depreciated between 2001 and 2007. Second, the link between the U.S. current account and the global savings account is also weak. The U.S. current account deficit started to deteriorate in the early 1990s, and continued to do so when the global savings rate decreased between 1998 and 2003. Third, there is no clear link between the global savings rate and real interest rate. Starting in the early 1990s, the real interest rate shows a consistent downward trend that shows no clear correlation with the behavior of the global savings rate. Fourth, an increase in global savings should show a fall in GDP. Note that the savings glut hypothesis rests on the assumption that savings are used to acquire financial assets rather than spend on the production of new goods. GDP, however, shows steady growth rates.

Borio and Disyatat (2011) argue that the reason why the savings glut hypothesis has been supported despite the contradiction of the stylized facts discussed above is to not distinguish between savings and financing. Consider a closed economy without savings. This economy may have no savings (all output is consumed). But, as long as there is production of goods and services, financing is taking place. If this closed economy (i.e. the whole word) is separated into different regions, then the trade account will show an inflow and outflow of funds that is not the result of savings but of trade. In an increasingly globalized economy, this flow of financing funds would also increase. In short, a current account deficit, which implies a capital account surplus, does not mean that borrowing is increasing. A capital account surplus can be the result of foreign direct investment, of asset purchases, or of a bank account deposit. Borrowing is one way to explain a capital account surplus, not the only one. Bernanke (2005), however, holds that when "U.S. receipts from its sales of exports and other current payments are insufficient to cover the cost of U.S. imports and other payments to foreigners, U.S. households, firms, and government on net *must borrow* the difference on international capital markets" (emphasis added).

The savings glut hypothesis may explain the initial phase of the boom, but empirical evidence does not support the thesis that the whole process was driven by this phenomenon. However, the argument that a general loose monetary policy by major central banks played a central role in the housing bubble that lead to the 2008 financial crisis does not overrule the savings glut hypothesis as a first driver of prices and interest rates before 2001. But other explanations are required to explain the size and timing of the housing bubble. For example, as shown in Figure 6.2, the rise in house prices in the mid-1990s in the U.S. also matches key regulatory changes discussed above (See "The building of the crisis" earlier in this chapter).

In short, the arguments that see central banks as a required component to understand the 2008 crisis can be summarized as follows (McKinnon, 2010; O'Driscoll, 2009; Schwartz, 2007, 2009; Selgin, Beckworth, and Bahadir, 2015; Taylor, 2009; White, 2008). The Federal Reserve, the supplier of the world currency reserved, was deluded to think that its policy was on track due to the lack of high inflation. Inflation did not rise for two reasons. The first one is an increase in productivity gains that, *ceteris paribus*, would have produced good deflation. The result was *implicit* inflation concealed behind a stable price level. The second reason is the reaction of other major central banks to the Federal Reserve's low interest rate policy. To avoid appreciation of their currencies and damage to their exports, other central banks mimicked the Federal Reserve's monetary policy. The increase in liquidity was channeled to assets outside the scope of the GDP deflator or CPI such as the price of houses or stocks and bonds (and, arguably, commodities with their prices defined in the international markets). Additionally, imports by the United States became elastic because the excess of liquidity could be allocated to imports, increasing the quantity consumed rather than the price level. As pointed out by Ahrend, Cournède, and Price (2008), those countries that, with respect to Taylor's rule, followed a looser monetary policy are also the ones facing larger housing bubbles. The problem was not so much a savings glut, where savings is postponed consumption, as it was a liquidity glut. The excess of liquidity was the outcome of major central banks' monetary policies.

Notes

1 See the discussion in Allison (2012) and White (2008).
2 The Federal Reserve Board. Household Debt Service and Financial Obligations Ratios. Release data. December 13, 2013.
3 While quantitative easing refers to a monetary expansion that steps outside the conventional assets purchased in open market operations, qualitative easing is when the monetary authority targets specific assets.
4 There were in total three of these institutions, Maiden Lane I, II, and III. Their purpose was to financially assist the bailout of Bear Stearns, American Investment Group (AIG), and AIG's credit default swap division respectively.
5 Bernanke (2015, p. 215) argues that Bear Stearns was *too interconnected to fail* and not so much *too big to fail*.
6 A thrift institution is a financial firm that primarily works with household savings. Savings and loans associations are a type of thrift institution.
7 The original budget was of $700 billion. The Dodd–Frank Wall Street Reform and Consumer Protection Act reduced the amount to $475 billion.
8 Caballero, Farhi, and Gourinchas (2008) argue that the issue is not an excess of savings, but a shortage of investment opportunities (financial assets) that lead savers to look for financial opportunities in developing countries.

References

Ahrend, R., Cournède, B., and Price, R. (2008). Monetary Policy, Market Excesses and Financial Turmoil. *Economics Department Working Paper No. 597*. Basel: OECD.

Allison, J. A. (2012). *The Financial Crisis and the Free Market Cure: Why Pure Capitalism Is the World Economy's Only Hope*. New York: McGraw-Hill.

Bernanke, B. S. (1983). Nonmonetary Effects of the Financial Crisis in the Propagation of the Great Depression. *American Economic Review*, 73.(3): 257–276.

Bernanke, B. S. (1988). Monetary Policy Transmission: Through Money or Credit? *Federal Reserve Bank of Philadelphia Business Review*, September: 3–11.

Bernanke, B. S. (2005). *Sandridge Lecture: The Global Savings Glut and the U.S. Current Account Deficit*. Richmond, VA: Virginia Association of Economics.

Bernanke, B. S. (2013). *The Federal Reserve and the Financial Crisis*. Princeton and Oxford: Princeton University Press.

Bernanke, B. S. (2015). *The Courage to Act: A Memoir of a Crisis and Its Aftermath*. New York and London: W. W. Norton & Company.

Bernanke, B. S., and Gertler, M. (1995). Inside the Black Box: The Credit Channel of Monetary Policy Transmission. *Journal of Economic Perspectives*, 9.(4): 27–48.

Blanchard, O. (2014). Where Danger Lurks. *Finance & Development*, (September): 28–31.

Blanchard, O. (2016). Do DSGE Models Have a Future? *Policy Brief No. 16–11*. Washington, DC: Peterson Institute for International Economics.

Blanchard, O., Dell'Ariccia, G., and Mauro, P. (2010). Rethinking Macroeconomic Policy. *Journal of Money, Credit and Banking*, 42.(6): 199–215.

Blau, B. M. (2017). Lobbying, Political Connections and Emergency Lending by the Federal Reserve. *Public Choice*, 172.(3–4): 333–358.

Borio, C., and Disyatat, P. (2011). Global Imbalances and the Financial Crisis: Link or no Link? *BIS Working Papers No. 346*. Basel: Bank for International Settlements.

Bracke, T., and Fidora, M. (2012). The Macro-Financial Factors Behind the Crisis: Global Liquidity Glut or Global Savings Glut? *The North American Journal of Economics and Finance*, 23.(2): 185–202.

Caballero, R. J. (2010). Macroeconomics after the Crisis: Time to Deal with the Pretense-of-Knowledge Syndrome. *Journal of Economic Perspectives*, 24.(4): 85–102.

Caballero, R. J., Farhi, E., and Gourinchas, P.-O. (2008). An Equilibrium Model of "Global Imbalances" and Low Interest Rates. *American Economic Review*, 98.(1): 358–393.

Dixit, A. K., and Pyndick, R. S. (1994). *Irreversible Investment*. Princeton: Princeton University Press.

Goodhart, C. A. E. (1987). Why Do Banks Need a Central Bank? *Oxford Economic Papers*, 39.(1): 75–89.

Higgs, R. (2009). Regime Uncertainty. *The Independent Review*, 1.(4): 561–590.

Hogan, T. L., Le, L., and Salter, A. W. (2015). Ben Bernanke and Bagehot's Rule. *Journal of Money, Credit and Banking*, 47.(2–3): 333–348.

Hume, M., and Sentance, A. (2009). The Global Credit Boom: Challenges for Macroeconomics and Policy. *Journal of International Money and Finance*, 28.(8): 1426–1461.

Hummel, J. R. (2011). Ben Bernanke versus Milton Friedman. The Federal Reserve's Emergence as the U.S. Economy's Central Planner. *The Independent Review*, 15.(4): 485–518.

Keen, S. (2018). The WHO Warns of Outbreak of Virulent New "Economic Reality" Virus. *Review of Keynesian Economics*, 5.(1): 107–111.

McKinnon, R. (2010). Rehabilitating the Unloved Dollar Standard. *Asian-Pacific Economic Literature*, 24.(2): 1–18.

O'Driscoll, G. P. J. (2009). Money and the Present Crisis. *Cato Journal*, 29.(1): 167–186.

Romer, P. (forthcoming). The Trouble with Macroeconomics. *The American Economist*.

Ryou, J.-W. (2009). What Is Driving Economic Imbalances? The Global Savings Glut Hypothesis Revisited. *East Asian Economic Review*, 13.(2): 3–36.

Schwartz, A. J. (2007). The Role of Monetary Policy in the Face of the Crises. *Cato Journal*, 27.(2): 157–163.

Schwartz, A. J. (2009). Origins of the Financial Market Crisis of 2008. *Cato Journal*, 29.(1): 19–23.

Selgin, G. A. (2017). IOER and Banks' Demand for Reserves, Yet Again. Retrieved December 7, 2017, from https://www.alt-m.org/2017/06/01/ioer-and-banks-demand-for-reserves-yet-again/

Selgin, G. A., Beckworth, D., and Bahadir, B. (2015). The Productivity Gap: Monetary Policy, the Subprime Boom, and the Post-2001 Productivity Surge. *Journal of Policy Modeling*, 37.(2): 189–207.

Stiglitz, J. E. (2011). Rethinking Macroeconomics: What Failed, and How to Repair It. *Journal of the European Economic Association*, 9.(4): 591–645.

Sumner, S. (2012). The Case for Nominal GDP Targeting. *Mercatus Research*. Arlington: George Mason University.

Taylor, J. B. (2009). *Getting Off Track*. Stanford: Hoover Institute Press.

White, L. H. (2008). How Did We Get into This Financial Mess? *Briefing Papers No.110*. Washington, DC: Cato Institute.

7 Monetary reforms toward nominal income targeting

Introduction

Previous chapters discussed the difference between actively setting and aiming at a monetary objective and having the target be spontaneously produced by the market. As long as a central bank aims to mimic the outcome of a competitive market in money and banking, then the literature of free banking points to nominal income stabilization rather than price level stabilization.

However, the presence itself of a central bank distorts the functioning of a free-banking regime. This raises the question of how a central bank can achieve the same result when the market process that produces the required information is now working differently to a free-banking scenario. Central banks need to find replacements for the missing information that free banking provides. Rather than finding substitutes to use as a diagnosis tool of monetary policy (such as inflation), a more general approach would be to produce an institutional reform that would move the market closer to a free-banking scenario or nominal income stabilization. A new institutional design would put in place the incentives for the market to move toward monetary equilibrium by itself without the need to rely so much on the efficiency of central banks.

This chapter discusses four institutional reforms that give more participation to market participants and put less weight on central banking efficiency. The discussed reforms are the feasibility of returning to the gold standard, a fiat-based free-banking regime, currency competition, and the development of an NGDP futures market.

Is going back to the gold standard feasible?

Given the worldwide failure of major central banks to foresee the 2008 crisis and to successfully manage the downturn, the idea of returning to the gold standard gained momentum. During the financial crisis central banks were seen as oblivious to how and why the crisis was unfolding the way it did and were too slow to react to the unfolding events. In addition, the complexities of the financial instruments involved in this crisis made the situation even harder to understand, not only by the median voter, but also by the politician in search of electoral support. There is a distance, however, between *desiring* to go back to the gold standard and *being able* to do so.[1]

The classic gold standard, where each country has a national central bank that issues banknotes convertible to gold, can be seen as a *sticky* free-banking system. Each country, instead of having a number of issuer banks, has one *de facto* state bank. These national central banks are subject to public choice issues such as political pressures that can ultimately deviate their behavior from the optimal policy. This situation can lead, for instance, to an increase in moral hazard behavior by the rest of the financial market. Besides these public choice issues, the presence of a unique central bank of issue affects the adverse clearing mechanism that under free banking inform banks on the stance of their policy. The *macro* result of banks competing under this regime results in monetary equilibrium. Despite its stickiness, the gold standard has the advantage over a fiat currency regime of aiming at the right target and restricting the government's monetization of deficit. From an institutional point of view, the gold standard is like a constitutional norm that constrains the monetization of fiscal deficits. Salter (2014) argues that other monetary regimes, such as free banking and NGDP targeting, can also have self-enforcing properties.

A number of objections are usually raised against gold standard itself. Probably the most common one is that under gold standard, money supply is subject to random discoveries (exogenous shocks) of gold. While it is possible that under gold standard random and accidental discoveries of gold can affect money supply, it is not the case that money supply is determined only randomly. An increase in the demand of gold raises its price, which incentivizes an increase in gold mining activities, and therefore the search for new gold sources. The case of a price-driven increase in the search of gold sources is an endogenous change in the supply of gold. These mining activities are contributing to reach monetary equilibrium. Not every discovery of gold should be understood as an exogenous shock that disrupts the money market.

Some discoveries, such as those of the mid-1850s in California, Australia, and New Zealand can be considered exogenous. But other gold discoveries later in the 1800s were endogenous as they were driven by the high price of gold. It is true that in *theory*, a central bank can manage a money supply free of random shocks in a less costly way than under the gold standard. But this comparison gets too close to the Nirvana Fallacy, where the gold standard as it is in the real world is compared with an ideal central bank rather than with the real and known performance of these monetary institutions. Other concerns about the gold standard such as producing harmful deflation, the need for a lender of last resort, and producing bank runs have already been dealt with in Chapter 1.

It has also been pointed out that the gold standard is a costly regime since gold has to be mined, processed, and then stored in banks. A monetary regime based on fiat money can offer a similar procedure in a significantly less costly way. It is cheaper to "print" money than to mine, process, transport, and keep gold safe. Friedman (1951, 1960) estimates that the cost of acquiring the required gold for an economy that in average grows 2% every year would be 2.5% of GDP. According to Friedman's result, the gold standard, even if it works efficiently, would be too expensive. It is plausible that a fiat-money-based regime, even if somewhat less efficient than the gold standard, would be considerably cheaper, freeing a large amount of resources to produce new goods and services.

Friedman's result, however, is significantly inflated for two reasons (White, 1999b, pp. 42–48). First, Friedman assumes that banks hold 100% reserves on bank deposits rather than fractional reserves. Second, Friedman assumes 100% reserves for M2, which also includes *non-demand* deposits such as time deposits. Using historical cases of free banking as a guide to a more realistic calculation, White finds that the actual cost of gold was one fiftieth of Friedman's estimation. A well-working free-banking regime, such as the one in Scotland, carried a gold cost of 0.05 percent of GNP. This is not a prohibitive cost to pay for a stable monetary regime. Returning to the gold standard would not impose a significant cost to the economy.

There are also issues to consider, rather than on gold standard itself, on the *transition* from fiat money to a gold standard regime. Note, first, that returning to a gold standard regime, where each country's fiat currency would become convertible to gold, would not require a change in the currency denomination already familiar to producers and consumers such as the dollar, the British Pound, etc. What would be defined is the amount of gold each new dollar in circulation will be a claimable to. Just as when transitioning away from the gold standard, the look of the currency can remain mostly unchanged, but the fiat currency paper would be swapped for convertible banknotes. In addition, there is no problem such as whether or not there is enough gold to reinstate a gold standard regime. Certainly, defining the new convertibility ratio can prove challenging, but this is a different issue to whether or not such convertibility ratio exists.

It has also been pointed out that the price of gold is too unstable and, therefore, a gold standard regime would have an erratic money supply. This reading is based on the conception that gold standard is a regime under which the central bank fixes the price of gold. As was mentioned in the first chapter, the gold standard does not fix the price of gold any more than a check fixes the price of the underlying currency, or a bond fixes the price of its unit of payment. Under the gold standard, the dollar is not base money, gold is. What the gold standard does is define convertibility between IOUs and gold. Under this regime, the central bank banknotes are an indirect way of using gold in a similar way to a check being an indirect way of using the dollar (or any other currency). Present day fiat money is not convertible to gold, and therefore there is a *price* between fiat money and gold. The volatility on the price of gold has less to do with the gold standard being unstable and more with gold being used to hedge against the higher inflation produced by the fiat-money regime. The behavior of the price of gold outside of a gold standard regime should not be used as a benchmark of what conditions gold would have under a regime where gold is money.

The most difficult challenge to return to a gold standard is political (White, 2008). The gold standard is not a national monetary regime, but an international monetary arrangement *without* a central supplier of base money. All the countries under the gold standard are plugged into the same money network. The difference across countries is not that they have different base money, but that different money *substitutes* (convertible banknotes) circulate inside each region. A successful return to the gold standard requires major countries to coordinate their return to the gold standard and also be willing to give up a centrally managed supply of base money. A unilateral return to the gold standard, where only one central bank issues convertible banknotes to gold would not produce the large-scale benefits of this system. For instance, clearing among central banks against gold claims would not occur. The biggest challenge to return to the gold standard (assuming it is convenient) is political rather than technical.

A fiat-based free-banking regime

Besides the political challenge of a coordinated return to the gold standard by major central banks, this monetary regime carries the *stigma* of being a poor institutional choice in the economics profession. A return to the gold standard also faces the challenge of transitioning from gold not being money to gold being money. Selgin (1988, Chapter 11) offers an alternative monetary reform based on the U.S. dollar. This reform has the advantage, over gold, of being built over the U.S. dollar which is already used as money. Selgin's proposal can be separated in three parts.

The first part consists in freezing the supply of U.S. dollars. To make this monetary rule free of political intervention, the Federal Reserve should be at least *de facto* closed. For instance, the institution can remain open with some regulatory powers or a financial overseeing role, but the Federal Open Markets Committee that decides and carries monetary policy should be closed; this would also eliminate the possibility of monetary discretion. The institution of the Federal Reserve would remain, but its central banking powers of managing money supply will be eliminated. *Ceteris paribus*, freezing the supply of U.S. dollars means that money supply may not be able to adjust to changes in money demand as efficiently as it would be under a nominal income targeting rule well executed by a central bank. In addition, the clearing services could also be privatized. Private banks may open their own clearing houses where only solvent and well-managed banks are accepted to their *clearing club*. This way, clearing houses not only provide clearing services, but also become a quality check among members. A bank may be more inclined to lend money to another *clearing club* member than to a non-member bank. Being a member of the *clearing club* saves each bank the cost of being familiar with the financial situation of each potential party. It is a way to reduce the cost of acquiring information about other banks.

The second part of Selgin's reform mitigates the *inelastic* component of the money supply produced by freezing the supply of U.S. dollars. Under this reform, banks would be allowed to issue their own banknotes convertible to the U.S. dollar. In practical terms, this reform is a free-banking regime built on a fixed supply of U.S. dollars rather than on a variable amount of gold. The appeal of Selgin's reform is that the U.S. dollar has today a similar role to that of gold under free banking. Under this regime, like in gold-based free banking, changes in money demand can be matched by changes in private banknotes rather than in base money. Adjustments of money supply to money demand become market driven, rather than being the result of policy makers.

The third part of this reform deals with the problem of the U.S. dollar and private banknotes being a close (or even perfect) substitute with each other for day-to-day transactions. Namely, there is no advantage for consumers in carrying a private banknote over a U.S. dollar. In the case of gold, it is more pragmatic to deposit gold in the bank and carry convertible banknotes or a checkbook. This advantage is not present in the case of a banknotes convertible to a fiat currency with similar physical characteristics. Because of this, Selgin proposes replacing the frozen circulation of U.S. dollars with uncomfortable-to-use paper base money. The new U.S. dollars may have, for instance, different sizes and shapes that do not fit well in standard wallets. One bill may have the shape of a trapezoid, another one can have a circular form, a third one might be triangular, etc. Their appearance may also be modified so that they look less familiar to the everyday user of paper money. The familiar green of the U.S. dollar might be changed for colors such as yellow, red, blue, etc.

Selgin's proposal is less extreme than a plain return to the gold standard. This proposal, however, can still be considered politically inviable. Still, it should be noted that monetary regimes similar to this do exist in present times. Hogan (2012) studies the cases of Hong Kong, Scotland, and Northern Ireland. In these countries, some private banks issue their own banknotes convertible into their national currency. Also, in these countries private banknotes do have a significant market share of the transactions in their economies. The practice of supplying private banknotes is a profitable line of business for these banks that contributes to their financial stability as well. A movement toward a system like this would provide a more market-driven money supply, contributing to the monetary equilibrium of the economy, and also enhance the financial stability of the banks through the new source of revenue.

This reform need not be constrained to large economies. Economies smaller than the United States, and especially if they have troubled currencies, can benefit from a proposal like this one. Hanke (2001), Hanke and Schuler (1999a, 1999b), and Schuler and Hanke (2001) propose a similar arrangement for Argentina. During the 1990s, Argentina had an unorthodox currency board (Cachanosky and Ravier, 2015; Hanke, 2008). With the unorthodox currency board, Argentina was one step closer to implementing a reform like this one. After years of fiscal deficit, in late 2001 the Argentine government decided to default its sovereign debt. The 2001 crisis presented two alternatives. With a history of significant inflation rates, Argentina had the option to either become formally or informally dollarized. Argentina chose the latter. With no access to international financial markets, the new government decided to monetize its deficit leading, again, to increasing inflation rates.[2]

Finally, Selgin's proposal to fix the amount of U.S. dollars is unlikely to be the optimal behavior of base money under a fiat-based free-banking regime. The fact that the secondary creation of money in the form of convertible banknotes can contribute to changes in the supply of money does not mean that base money can remain frozen indefinitely. However, allowing for changes in the supply of U.S. dollars also means opening the door to even larger mistakes by policy makers. But Selgin's proposal does not claim to forbid other currencies to eventually become the new base money if the frozen U.S. dollar proves to be too inefficient. It will be up to the market, however, to manage such transition. Whether gold would be again chosen as money or another commodity such as gold is an outcome of the market process. Or, maybe, privately issued fiat (or digital) currencies become the money of choice to replace the U.S. dollar.

Currency competition

Independently, Hayek (1976) and Klein (1974) study an alternative monetary reform known as *currency competition*.[3] Shortly, the argument rests in the idea that in a competitive market of currency issuers, competition forces would keep suppliers of fiat money in check and the result would be stable money. This proposal offers an alternative approach to what later came to be the Euro Zone. Rather than having one currency for a number of countries, the currency competition proposal advocates for letting each fiat money freely compete across countries.

While currency competition is also a scenario of a free market of money and banking, there is a substantial difference between these two monetary regimes. The first and substantial difference is that under *currency competition*, issuer banks supply their own currency or base money instead of banknotes convertible to the *same* base money. This is an important difference with some relevant implications.

First, under free banking, the supply of base money such as gold is the result of a number of miners that compete with each other. There is no single supply of base money. In the case where free banking works with more than one base money, for instance if gold and silver circulate as money at the same time, then each one of these commodities is still supplied by a number of miners competing with each other. Under currency competition, however, each bank issues its own currency. Free banking has only one base money supplied by a number of producers. Currency competition has a number of fiat currencies each supplied by a unique bank.

This is a different issue from having a private stamp on gold coins that identify the miner or minting where a particular coin is coming from. Different suppliers of gold may mark their own coins, but all of them are supplying gold coins.[4] This is the analogous case of free banks issuing their own convertible banknotes with their brand identification while all banknotes are convertible to the same base money. Under currency competition, then, each bank is responsible for efficiently managing their own currency. If their currency is not efficiently managed, then its market share would fall in favor of a more stable currency issued by another bank. A similar but more *sticky* process is what we observe when economic agents of a country with a troubled currency save and price large purchases and investments in a foreign currency. The result is an informally *dollarized* economy. The currency competition proposal reduces this *stickiness* in favor of more competitive and flexible alternatives.

Under currency competition, banks would compete by stabilizing the purchasing power of their currencies with respect to a defined basket of goods.[5] Hayek imagines a scenario where different banks would specialize in different markets and therefore stabilize different baskets of goods. For instance, Hayekian banks in Europe may stabilize the price level of goods traded across European countries, and Hayekian countries in the United States would do the same with a basket of goods that better represent its pattern of consumption. Economic agents would not need to carefully study the balance of issuer banks, it would be sufficient to observe in the media how stable the purchasing power of each currency is. Some banks may specialize on the needs of large transactions, others on the needs of daily needs purchases, and so on.

Hayek's vision of a number of different currencies circulating at the same time and competing with each other assumes that money has a low network effect or that the chosen basket of goods of each bank is a strong focal point for different currency networks. As a network good, however, it is likely that one (or only a few) currencies would survive because the utility of a network good increases with the number of users connected to the network. Therefore, each economic agent would converge to use the same currency (even if it happens to not be the best currency). It is possible that, assuming Hayek's argument, a few different networks could co-exist built on different baskets of goods. But as long as the benefit of having different baskets of goods does not exceed the cost of opportunity of having a network, only one or a small number of currencies should be expected to circulate. Friedman (1984) challenges Hayek on this particular point arguing that economic agents are not likely to be sensitive enough to changes in the purchasing power of money to easily change currencies. Luther (2013) studies the case of stateless Somalia as *de fact* currency competition. With the fall of the Somali government, legal tender laws become ineffective and Somalis were free to use any currency of their choice. Luther finds that, in the case of Somalia, Friedman's point was a valid one. Somalis kept using their Somali shilling notes, and the currency competition scenario, as envisioned by Hayek, failed to develop. It is possible, then, that because of the network effects the currency used is inefficient and that therefore a central bank could provide a better currency than the market. The central bank could make sure that currency competition does not yield an inferior Nash equilibrium where all economic agents do not want to deviate from using a sub-optimal currency.

There is still another issue to consider in the case of currency competition. In this regime, issuer banks are not regular banks in the sense that each bank is the *primary* issuer of their own currency rather than the source of the *secondary* expansion of money. This is of relevance since the secondary creation of money occurs through liabilities such as a convertible banknote or a demand deposit. A regular bank has a contractual obligation with their depositors. But a Hayekian bank has no contractual obligation with their currency users. A Hayekian bank *promises* to keep the price level of a given basket of goods stable, but there is no contractual obligation to do so.

Because of this, issuer banks under currency competition face a time inconsistency type of situation (Kydland and Prescott, 1977). Once an issuer bank gains credibility about his efficiency to stabilize the price level of a given basket of goods, the bank has the incentive to increase the supply of its own currency and buy assets *before* the purchasing power of its currency is affected and it loses its clients. If the discount rate of the bank owners is high enough, this hyperinflation strategy would be chosen over a price level stability strategy. A Hayekian bank can follow this strategy because the bank would be breaking a promise, but not a contract, to its customers.

NGDP futures market

Sumner (1989; 2013) proposes the development of an NGDP futures market as a means to align market expectations with the Federal Reserve's NGDP target. A significant component of NGDP targeting is that NGDP and market expectations coincide such that there is neither an excess nor a shortage of a nominal income that will affect expenditures. Without a clear mechanism to reveal market expectation about the future of NGDP, the easiest way to make policy and expectations coincide is by targeting both the level and growth of NGDP in a stable fashion. NGDP should promptly return to its previous level and the growth rate of NGDP should always be the same. The development of an NGDP futures market would become both a source of information about market expectations for policy makers, and a new mechanism to execute and adjust changes in money supply. Futures markets with different instruments, such as a consumer price level, could also be designed.

An NGDP futures market would work in the following way. First, the central bank would define at period 0 the NGDP target for period 1 and issue "NGDP future" instruments. For convenience, the "NGDP future" instrument could trade at one dollar plus the NGDP difference between period 1 and period 0. If, for instance, by period 1 the central bank targets NGDP to be 5% above period 0, then the price of an NGDP future would be 1.05 dollars, the price at which the central bank would buy and sell unlimited numbers of NGDP futures. When period 1 arrives, all NGDP future instruments are liquidated with a value that reflects that actual change in NGDP. If NGDP actually grew 3%, then those investors who hold a *long* position will make a gain of 2 cents per instrument and those investors who held a *short* position would lose two cents per instrument. With the price of NGDP futures fixed at the NGDP target, investors would reveal their expectations by going *long* or *short* on NGDP future instruments.

The profit opportunity incentivized the involvement of well-informed participants willing to bear the risk of making a loss. This incentive mechanism contributes for more accurate expectations to be revealed. In this sense, this futures market has a similar characteristic to that of the prediction markets where participants bet on an outcome. The price of such bet, for instance whether the incumbent or the challenger would win an election, reveals market expectations that are usually more accurate than polls where contributors are not sorted by expertise and they do not have any stake on whether their prediction is right or wrong.

With an NGDP futures market, then, the central bank announces the target of NGDP and the behavior of the futures market participants reveals whether the market expects NGDP to miss the target in either direction. These market expectations need to be translated into a monetary policy that would correct NGDP deviations from its target until NGDP expectations and target are again matched. This link can be constructed by having open market operations follow the purchase (*long* position) and sell (*short* position) of NGDP futures. The purchase (sell) of an NGDP future instrument would trigger a thousand (or million, etc.) dollars sell (buy) through open market operations. This means that if investors in the NGDP futures market expect NGDP to be above its target, investors moving to a *short* position would trigger a tightening of monetary policy. Inversely, investors moving to a *long* position would trigger a loosening of the monetary policy.

Note that the central bank decides the *target*, but it is the investors who are the ones deciding *which* policy would hit the target. Open market operations are decided by the investors, not by the policy makers. This reduces the burden of knowledge and *alertness* required by policy makers by relying on well-informed economic agents acting *in* the market. The central bank, however, still remains responsible for choosing the right variable and the right target. While these are not minor issues, a futures market in general increases the information available to market participants and provides a mechanism to correct monetary policy mistakes. Monetary policy is decided by a larger pool of experts rather than relying only on the central bank experts.

Another way to think about the NGDP future market is, following Sumner's (2013, p. 20) analogy, as a road guardrail. Ideally, a road guardrail would never be needed, but this does not mean they should not be installed on a twisting mountain road. Sumner argues that during the 2008 crisis an NGPD futures market would have provided profit opportunities to market participants and a policy correction mechanism that would have softened the crisis. But without this market, market participants have no means of profiting from (and therefore correcting) the policy in place. The Federal Reserve could not learn nor correct its mistake in time.

Finally, Bernanke and Woodford (1997) point to a "circularity" or "simultaneity" problem under inflation targeting. This circularity occurs when the central bank and the market are watching each other to define what the level of inflation will be. The central bank uses private-sector inflation forecasts to inform their policy. But the private sector is trying to forecast what inflation the central bank will produce, which in turn depends on the private-sector forecast. Under inflation targeting, the central bank uses the private-sector forecast as input information to decide its own monetary policy. If market forecasts are trying to guess the policy of the central bank, then this information would be inaccurate. Because of this, Bernanke and Woodford argue that central banks need to rely on structural models beside market forecasts. However, under NGDP targeting, as Sumner argues, the target is decided by the central bank, but the policy is decided by the market. This means there is not a "circularity" as in the case of inflation targeting.

Notes

1 In 1953, shortly after Bretton Woods in 1944, Mises (1912) adds a "Monetary Reconstruction" discussion to his *The Theory of Money and Credit* . Mises's proposal consists of returning to banknote convertibility with a marginal 100% reserve requirement (applicable to *new* deposits). Contrary to some misconceptions, Mises's proposal calls for a 100% marginal reserve requirement for *issuer* banks (central banks) and major commercial banks, but not to the whole banking system. See Cachanosky (2012), and White (1992).
2 Cachanosky and Ravier (2015) offer an updated version of this reform that consists of closing down the Argentine central bank and moving to U.S. dollar-based free banking in Argentina as proposed by Selgin and studied by Hogan.
3 See also Nash (2002) *Ideal Money*.
4 Selgin (2008) offers a historical study of private mining of coins.
5 This implies a deviation from Hayek's rule by Hayek himself. For an analysis see White (1999a).

References

Bernanke, B. S., and Woodford, M. (1997). Inflation Forecast and Monetary Policy. *Journal of Money, Credit and Banking*, 29.(4 (November, Part 2)): 653–684.

Cachanosky, N. (2012). Mises on Fractional Reserves: A Review of Huerta de Soto's Argument. *New Perspectives on Political Economy*, 7.(2): 203–230.

Cachanosky, N., and Ravier, A. O. (2015). A Proposal of Monetary Reform for Argentina: Flexible Dollarization with Free Banking. *The Independent Review*, 19.(3): 397–426.

Friedman, M. (1951). Commodity-Reserve Currency. *Journal of Political Economy*, 59.(3): 203–232.

Friedman, M. (1960). *A Program for Monetary Stability*. New York: Fordham University Press.

Friedman, M. (1984). Currency Competition: A Skeptical View. In P. Salin (Ed.), *Currency Competition and Monetary Union* (pp. 42–46). Boston: Martinus Nijhoff Publishers.

Hanke, S. H. (2001). Argentina Endgame. Couple Dollarization with Free Banking. *Foreign Policy Briefing No. 67*. Washington, DC: Cato Institute.

Hanke, S. H. (2008). Why Argentina Did Not Have a Currency Board? *Central Banking Journal*, 18.(3): 56–58.

Hanke, S. H., and Schuler, K. (1999a). A Dollarization Blueprint for Argentina. *Foreign Policy Briefing No. 52*. Washington, DC: Cato Institute.

Hanke, S. H., and Schuler, K. (1999b). A Monetary Constitution for Argentina. *Cato Journal*, 18.(3): 405–419.

Hayek, F. A. (1976 [2007]). *Denationalisation of Money*. London: The Institute of Economic Affairs.

Hogan, T. L. (2012). Competition in Currency. *Policy Analysis No. 698*, 1–53. Washington, DC: Cato Institute.

Klein, B. (1974). The Competitive Supply of Money. *Journal of Money, Credit and Banking*, 6.(November): 423–453.

Kydland, F. E., and Prescott, E. C. (1977). Rules Rather than Discretion: The Inconsistency of Optimal Plans. *Journal of Political Economy*, 85.(3): 473–492.

Luther, W. J. (2013). Friedman Versus Hayek on Private Outside Monies: New Evidence for the Debate. *Economic Affairs*, 33.(1): 127–135.

Mises, L. von. (1912 [1981]). *The Theory of Money and Credit*. Indianapolis: Liberty Fund.

Nash, J. F. (2002). Ideal Money. *Southern Economic Journal*, 69.(1): 4–11.

Salter, A. W. (2014). Is There a Self-enforcing Monetary Constitution? *Constitutional Political Economy*, 25.(3): 280–300.

Schuler, K., and Hanke, S. H. (2001). How to Dollarize in Argentina, 1–46. Retrieved from http://www.cato.org/sites/cato.org/files/articles/schuler-hanke011231.pdf

Selgin, G. A. (1988). *The Theory of Free Banking*. Lanham: CATO Institute and Rowman & Littlefield.

Selgin, G. A. (2008). *Good Money*. University of Chicago Press and The Independent Institute.

Sumner, S. (1989). Using Futures Instrument Prices to Target Nominal Income. *Bulletin of Economic Research*, 41.(2): 157–162.

Sumner, S. (2013). A Market-Driven Nominal GDP Targeting Regime. *Mercatus Research*. Arlington: George Mason University.

White, L. H. (1992). Mises on Free-Banking and Fractional Reserves. In J. W. Robbins and M. Spangler (Eds), *A Man of Principle. Essays in Honor of Hans F. Sennholz* (pp. 517–533). Grove City: Grove City College Press.

White, L. H. (1999a). Hayek's Monetary Theory and Policy: A Critical Reconstruction. *Journal of Money, Credit and Banking*, 31.(1): 109–120.

White, L. H. (1999b). *The Theory of Monetary Institutions*. Oxford: Basil Blackwell.

White, L. H. (2008). Is the Gold Standard Still the Gold Standard among Monetary Systems? *Briefing Papers No. 100*. Washington, DC: Cato Institute.

Index

For Product Safety Concerns and Information please contact our EU
representative GPSR@taylorandfrancis.com
Taylor & Francis Verlag GmbH, Kaufingerstraße 24, 80331 München, Germany

www.ingramcontent.com/pod-product-compliance
Ingram Content Group UK Ltd.
Pitfield, Milton Keynes, MK11 3LW, UK
UKHW020946180425
457613UK00019B/540